I PREFER THE

WINDOW SEAT

HAS THE AMERICAN CHURCH LEFT THE BATTLE?

A CONSIDERATION OF MATTHEW 9:35-38

TONY SCELLATO

WESTBOW
PRESS®
A DIVISION OF THOMAS NELSON
& ZONDERVAN

WestBow Press books may be ordered through booksellers or by contacting:

WestBow Press
A Division of Thomas Nelson & Zondervan
1663 Liberty Drive
Bloomington, IN 47403
www.westbowpress.com
844-714-3454

Scripture taken from the King James Version of the Bible

ISBN: 978-1-6642-0856-8 (sc)
ISBN: 978-1-6642-0855-1 (hc)
ISBN: 978-1-6642-0857-5 (e)

Library of Congress Control Number: 2020919890

Print information available on the last page.

WestBow Press rev. date: 10/16/2020

This book is dedicated to:
The children of Covenant House of St. Vincent
that God will allow us to serve and love.
We can't wait to meet you all!

And to:
My family
You have always given me the grace and encouragement
to chase the dreams God has put in my heart.

CONTENTS

³⁵ And Jesus went about all the cities and villages, teaching in their synagogues, and preaching the gospel of the kingdom, and healing every sickness and every disease among the people. ³⁶ But when he saw the multitudes, he was moved with compassion on them, because they fainted, and were scattered abroad, as sheep having no shepherd. ³⁷ Then saith he unto his disciples, The harvest truly is plenteous, but the labourers are few; ³⁸ Pray ye therefore the Lord of the harvest, that he will send forth labourers into his harvest.
(Matthew 9:35-38)

FOREWORD

I am known to some as Brother Peter, and I have been fortunate to live in three different continents including two years in Europe, nine years in Asia, and more than twenty-nine years in the United States. I have also spent nine years in the transcontinental region of the Middle East. Each of these countries has influenced my thinking, culture, and perspective on life. Additionally, my faith and ongoing growth as a Christian, have given me the perseverance, character, and hope to achieve what God has purposed in my life, and I praise God for that! I have a Bachelor's degree in Computer Engineering, a Master's degree in Information System Technology, and a Doctorate of Management in Organizational Leadership within Information System and Technology.

From the first time I met Tony, which was over 5 years ago, I could tell that there was something different about him. Tony is credible, funny, and glorifies God in everything he does. Jesus has commanded us to let our light shine before men, so that everyone may see our good works and glorify our Father which is in heaven (Matthew 5:16), and Tony is an exemplary example of being a light for Jesus. Tony's and my relationship strengthen us as brothers in Christ, especially in our journey to India, where the Lord was not only using us, but was teaching us individually and collaboratively on how to depend on Him for every simple need. Remember, God is most glorified when we are completely dependent on Him! At the beginning of this missionary journey, I thought that I could provide some assistance to God and to Tony on this trip. Quickly, I realized that even the things we are confident of in ourselves, are most effective when we are humbled and dependent on Him.

The Holy Spirit has used Tony tremendously in writing this book on how God was working in our lives through this journey. We may go with our agendas, or even with conviction and zeal for doing God's work, but if we are not led by the Holy Spirit, we are not glorifying God and His purpose to the fullest! God has used Tony to bring up a question we need to all be asking ourselves regularly. What seat do you prefer, a window or aisle? Paul says in the Bible that we need to test ourselves to make sure we are in the faith, and that Jesus Christ is indeed in us, unless we realize we have failed the test (2 Corinthians 13:5).

God is the same yesterday, today, and forever (Hebrews 13:8). The Ruach Ha-Kodesh, which is translated from Hebrew as the breath of Yahweh, has been given to us to guide us. So if we live by the Spirit, then let us also walk by the Spirit (Galatians 5:25). Just like the day God, through Moses, gave His people the law at Mt. Sinai, God has given His Word in our hearts and minds (Hebrews 10:16). So let us be led by the Spirit of God to know Him and to make Him known!

Blessings,
Brother Peter
Doctorate of Management in Organizational Leadership within Information System and Technology (DM/IST)

INTRODUCTION

A friend and I travelled to India in October, 2014. Our mission was to visit a few ministries with which I had been corresponding. I wanted to see, firsthand, the work they were doing in their respective areas of ministry to kids and pray about if God would have our ministry be involved in any way. In 2009, my wife and I started YES Ministries, a youth ministry focused on serving, evangelizing and discipling kids for Christ throughout the Caribbean region. Though involvement in India would be a completely different area for us, we were willing if it was where God wanted us.

As we boarded the plane in Chicago to begin the 8,000+ mile trip to Mumbai, India, Peter, my missionary traveling buddy, jokingly made the comment that was the inspiration for this book. We looked at our tickets to see which seats we had for our initial flight from Chicago, Illinois to Cincinnati, Ohio. I had the aisle seat and Peter had the window seat, on the small commuter jet. That is when Peter said to me, *"Go ahead, I'll take the aisle, though I prefer the window seat."* Immediately, God spoke to my heart saying, that's the picture of American Christianity today. You see, there is a big difference between the two seats. There really is! Being in the aisle seat truly forces you to see what is happening around you. People constantly on the move. You have to be alert so you don't get hit by the food cart or ready to listen to the guy across the aisle who wants to strike up a conversation. But, the window seat, oh, the window seat. You can tuck right into the window seat and simply drift off into each passing cloud. No worries, no cares. The world below seems so small and harmless. Someone even has to get your attention when it is time to eat or grab a coke!

Now, before you get the wrong impression of Peter, let me clarify. I am in no way saying that Peter's faith or walk with the Lord is lacking. It's quite the contrary. Peter is a man that seeks to do God's will, leads his family in a way pleasing to the Lord, and has great compassion toward those in need. Remember, I did say he said this jokingly! Though there are many today who are squarely in the battle, serving the Lord, and trying to impact this world for Jesus Christ, there is a changing trend, especially in American Christianity, that to me is alarming. It's a trend that seems to focus more on "me" first and then the multitudes second, if at all. Church is about me, my experience, my entertainment, my goodness and not about Christ, His glory, His worship, and His praise. It is we who are to come and worship the Lord, not come for the Lord to serve us, or dare I say, worship us. It is an alarming trend for this reason. Throughout the world, nations are impacted and influenced by America, what we do and say. Right or wrong, others look to America to lead, even in the area of Christianity, and so I pray we do so wisely and with caution. Take heed as Jesus would warn. It is alarming to me because I believe this softer gospel approach has led to a softer outlook on sin throughout the Christian community. You may disagree with my assessment of today's church, but all I ask is that you read the whole book, let me present my case, and if the Lord speaks to you, just be obedient to Him. This book is not about me being right, it is simply a challenge from the Word of God for all of us, me included. Ask yourself, when it comes to the defense of the Gospel, am I part of the problem or, with God's power, will I be part of the solution? Read the scripture, study it, and allow God to speak to you as He sees fit. I would agree, we have no greater example of love, kindness, patience, and compassion than our Lord and Savior, Jesus Christ. But, I also know when it comes to the topic of sin, Christ is uncompromising. I didn't say unforgiving, but He is uncompromising. But why? That's easy, it is because of what sin reveals about us. Sin reveals our rejection of Jesus – "If I had not come and spoken unto them, they had not had sin: but now they have no cloke for their sin." (John 15:22). Sin reveals our hatred of Jesus and the Father – "If I had not done among them the works which none other man did, they had not had sin: but now have they both seen and hated both me and my Father." (John 15:24). Sin reveals our selfish, religiously superior attitude. We know better than God – "Jesus said unto them, If ye were blind, ye should have no sin: but now ye say, We see; therefore your sin remaineth." (John 9:41). This is where I believe the problem lies. The Christian community, in its desire to teach or show the love of God, has begun to compromise on sin, even justify it. It's not even about what scripture says anymore. Often, it is about how we feel. What is sin to me may not be to you. And, if it's for a good reason or cause, God will be ok with it. He won't be mad! We say we don't want to be offensive, be all things to all people (I believe we have misused and taken this out of context), but it is understanding our sin problem, how it separates us from God, and that Jesus died to pay the penalty for our sin and rose again, the Gospel, that brings one to the point of salvation. That is why Jesus never compromised, because there cannot be a compromise. To compromise literally leads people away from God. It was that lost condition of man the angels proclaimed was Jesus' purpose for coming to earth – "And she shall bring forth a son, and thou shalt call his name JESUS: for he shall save his people from their sins." (Matthew 1:21). It was that lost condition that caused Jesus, in our text, to be moved with compassion. Jesus is our example of how to live the Christian life. If the lost moved Him to action, should they not move us as well? That is a rhetorical question. Obviously, the answer is YES, it should move us! I believe Jesus would choose the aisle seat, where the action is, and not slide into the window seat and gaze at the clouds as they pass by. Now, the aisle seat is definitely not comfortable, it is hard and often trying, and is absolutely a dangerous place to sit, but it is the seat God has commanded us to sit in.

So, you may be asking, what does the window seat really have to do with Christianity? Well, I hope through the pages of this book it will be clear to you, that you will be challenged to think about which "seat" you prefer to sit in. In this book, we will consider what it is that Jesus is asking of us, His disciples, today through the lens of Matthew 9:35-38

"And Jesus went about all the cities and villages, teaching in their synagogues, and preaching the gospel of the kingdom, and healing every sickness and every disease among the people. (36) But when he saw the multitudes, he was moved with compassion on them, because they fainted, and were scattered abroad, as sheep having no shepherd. (37) Then saith he unto his disciples, The harvest truly is plenteous, but the labourers are few; (38) Pray ye therefore the Lord of the harvest, that he will send forth labourers into his harvest."

And then as we follow His lead and begin to live as Jesus lived, you and I will better "see" and be "moved" (Matthew 9:36) with compassion to a life of action (Matthew 9:38, Mark 16:15, Matthew 28:19).

At the end of each chapter, you will see the phrase, Pray Through. I encourage you to pray through the scripture given. By praying through God's Word, you are literally praying God's heart.

What about you? What will your answer be? Are you still undecided? Not sure about the aisle seat? Will it still be, "that's ok, I prefer the window seat". Destination to be determined. On behalf of, well me, I'd like to say, Welcome aboard!

CHAPTER 1

Final Boarding Call for Flight #6145

"And Jesus went about all the cities and villages,"
— MATTHEW 9:35 —

October 2, 2014, 2:00 a.m. The alarm goes off. Though excited about what's ahead, I have to admit, it was still a slow roll out of bed. I'm more the type that is still up at 2:00 a.m., not getting up at 2:00 a.m.! After months of planning and years of conversing with local ministries, today was the day I would embark on my sixteen day trip to India. As the slightly cooler shower water, for waking purposes, began to do its job, thoughts started flooding my mind. This was my first time traveling to India. Even with today's technology, I had never actually spoken to any of the ministry leaders I was going to meet. We had only messaged through Facebook. But, I still believed God was opening the door and leading us. What would it be like? What would I see and experience? Please don't let it be a cobra! What did God have in store? Are the people I am going to meet legit or crazy? You can only learn so much through Facebook, so, yeah, the thought crossed my mind. God, please use us while we are there. God, show us Your will. I double checked my bag to make sure I wasn't forgetting anything and at 2:45 a.m. I gently, and I mean gently, woke my wife. She would be dropping me off at my friend Peter's house. Peter, an American citizen, but born in India, would be traveling with me on this scout trip. Already missing them, I guess just something a parent feels, I hugged and kissed my kids goodbye and we headed off. It would be sixteen days before I saw them again. It was easily, the longest we have ever been apart. On our team trips to the Caribbean, we always go as a family, but on scout trips, I typically go alone and the trips are usually three to five days in length.

It's 3:15 a.m. as we pulled into the driveway at Peter's house. His wife, whom I presume he woke gently too, was going to drop us at our first stop, the bus stop. At 4:00 a.m. we boarded the MegaBus, leaving downtown Indianapolis and headed for Chicago. Let me stop and say something for those who believe missions is all excitement and exotic places. Think again! Missions is not a vacation. It is not about our comfort or pleasure. It's all about the Gospel! It's all for His glory! So, how do you maximize your funds to proclaim the Gospel and to be a blessing to local ministries through offerings? You take uncomfortable and slightly (or maybe a tad above slightly) smelly buses at 4:00 a.m. to another city to catch a flight and save $800. Does it always work out this way? No, but are you willing if that's what it takes? Let me add to something I stated earlier. Missions is not a vacation, *it's better!*

The sun was coming up as the bus pulled into downtown Chicago. It is 7:30 a.m. With luggage in hand, we made our way through the crowd of people making their way to work, to an area where we could hail a cab and head out to O'Hare International Airport for our early afternoon flight. Our taxi driver was a young lady from Kazakhstan. She was attending college in Chicago and drove a taxi to help pay her way through school. I was really impressed with her work ethic, but I think I was even more impressed with her driving skill! After several hours sitting in the airport, another one of the exciting aspects of missions, the call to board flight #6145 came. Cincinnati, Ohio here we come. Yep, you heard me right. Our first flight was to Cincinnati, Ohio. We just road a bus three and a half hours to Chicago to catch a one hour flight to Cincinnati, which is an hour and a half from Indianapolis. But, remember, we saved $800! I LOVE MISSIONS! From Cincinnati we flew nine hours to Paris, France. From Paris, another nine hours to Bombay (now known as Mumbai), India, arriving just before midnight local time. We collected our bags, exchanged some US dollars to Indian rupees and then located some of Peter's family who were waiting to welcome us just outside the airport. After hugs and a little small talk, Peter and I loaded our belongings onto a motorized rickshaw that would take us to his aunt's apartment. It is now 2:00 am. We arrived to a huge dinner awaiting us. Peter's aunt said she knew we would be hungry. It's 2:00 a.m. and I am sitting down for dinner! My body was really confused! I had forgotten what jet-lag felt like. After we ate, we decided to lie down for awhile and get some rest. Sounds good, right? Until I realize that in this bed, that may be queen size, but probably smaller, would be me, Peter and his cousin. Hey, this is missions! This is how we roll! When I awoke, I was quickly reminded, that when you allow God to use you to impact people for Him, you get the attention of satan (I refuse to capitalize his name).

When I woke up, and I was so tired, I immediately felt very anxious. Peter and his cousin were gone. I found out a little later that they had taken the train to go see another aunt before we had to fly out that afternoon. I began to have these feelings of being all alone. I was in a country I didn't know and I didn't know anyone. What if something happened to me? I had been cautioned not to travel to certain parts of India and to be careful in certain areas where we would be traveling because there were spots where radical Islam was prevalent. What if they knew I was there, broke in to the apartment, and kidnapped me? I'm telling you, the devil was messing with me bad! I think about how he tried that with Jesus after Jesus had been in the wilderness for 40 days. Jesus was hungry, and I'm sure pretty tired. The devil still uses the same tricks today. Nothing new!

Anyway, I was beginning to get a little shaken and, at one moment, even thought, *I need to get back to the airport and get home.* This isn't how you feel when you are on vacation. This is the mission's battlefield! I walked out and talked with Peter's aunt for a while and am so thankful that God began to comfort my heart as only He can. "Blessed be God, even the Father of our Lord Jesus Christ, the Father of mercies, and the God of all comfort, Who comforteth us in all our tribulation, that we may be able to comfort them which are in any trouble, by the comfort wherewith we ourselves are comforted of God." (2 Corinthians 1:3-4).

Aren't you so thankful for those verses? I wasn't thinking about those verses at that time, but I sure am glad that the God of those verses showed Himself faithful to do what He promised He would.

After spending the day in Mumbai, Peter and I were excited to catch our early evening flight to Hyderabad. We were scheduled to spend the first three days in Hyderabad with Pastor Wilson Saripalli. You might say we traveled through many "cities and villages" from the time we left Indianapolis to the time we landed in Hyderabad, India.

What Jesus did was so simple. It can be summed up in one word… GO! In fact, you could say that was the essence of His ministry. Jesus was always going with the message He came to give. How do we know this? Well, we learn it from a conversation Jesus had with a young scribe who wanted to follow Him. "Now when Jesus saw great multitudes about him, he gave commandment to depart unto the other side. And a certain scribe came, and said unto him, Master, I will follow thee whithersoever thou goest. And Jesus saith unto him, The foxes have holes, and the birds of the air have nests; but the Son of man hath not where to lay his head." (Matthew 8:18-20). This young man was so excited about following Jesus. Who wouldn't be, right? Think of all the cool things he would get to see and experience. It would be like being on vacation all the time with the greatest show on earth. Big crowds, big miracles! Sign me up! Now, we don't know how the young scribe reacted, but we can take a good guess based on other accounts in scripture when Jesus shared how His ministry works. In this case, Jesus informs the young man that He is constantly on the go and as He is traveling around, He doesn't have any place to stay. No friends to hang with. No hotels to stay at. I picture Jesus telling this young man about finding a good smooth rock to use as a pillow while He sleeps in a field. Can't you see the excitement draining from this guys face? Wait a minute! If you have no place to stay, then that probably means you also won't have a good home cooked meal or an all you can eat buffet. Jesus, what do you eat? I mean, what rock star lives like this? Really? The answer is, the one who chooses the aisle seat. As the old workout saying goes, "No pain, no gain". The young scribe wanted all the blessing, but didn't want to work for it. He wanted the entertaining vacation that someone else was paying for. He wanted the window seat. Wake me up when we get there!

Jesus was very clear, it's called a command, we too are to GO (Matthew 28:19-20, Mark 16:15). You ever notice the things Jesus asks us to do were the same things He did? That's what a perfect example looks like. The message only gets out when the messenger goes out. Romans 10:14-15 tells us, "How then shall they call on him in whom they have not believed? And how shall they believe in him of whom they have not heard? And how shall they hear without a preacher? And how shall they preach, except they be sent? As it is written, How beautiful are the feet of them that preach the gospel of peace, and bring glad tidings of good things!" So, why is it then, that too often we want to Stop (red light) or slow down (yellow light) when we are to GO (green light)? Is it because the mission ahead looks so daunting? Is it because I don't feel like I can do it? Is it because I don't fully trust God in it? Is it because the window seat is much more comfortable? Ah, comfort! Isn't that what we want ministry to be? I know I do. Surprised? Hey, I struggle with these things too. The point of this book is so we can encourage each other in what God has called us to do, whatever and wherever that may be. We are all imperfect people trying to deliver a perfect message, the Gospel. Sometimes we need help because ministry isn't comfortable.

I want you to notice something about Jesus' ministry. Where exactly did Jesus "GO"? We've said that God commands us to go into all of the world and that is true. This book recounts a trip I took to India, that's true. I think it is safe to say I love foreign missions. Again, true. But, the Gospel message isn't just for foreign lands. It is for your backyard as well. What do I mean by that? Jesus spent the majority of His ministry in the area of Galilee, pretty much His backyard. This changes everything. As someone who has led foreign mission trips, I've heard a lot of excuses as to why someone doesn't go. It's too dangerous to leave the country. I don't like to fly. I can't afford it. And my all-time favorite, I don't feel God is calling me to do that. Seriously! You just told me you don't feel God is calling you to go tell someone about Jesus! Don't get me started about how I wanted to reply to that one. So fine, don't go to a foreign country. What about your own backyard?

Are you going there and if not, why not? The answer is, because our own backyard isn't comfortable either. It's just the nature of the Gospel ministry. When you deal with sinful people, which we all are, it's uncomfortable. I'm not sure why this is surprising to us. Isn't it exactly what Jesus told the young scribe?

So, how are we going to deal with this discomfort? We're going to prefer the window seat. We're going to make our Christianity, our churches, more comfortable. No, I'm not talking about replacing the pews with chairs, which I actually like. I don't care what you sit on. You can sit in a pew or a chair. You can sit on a couch or a bucket. I really don't care. If the Holy Spirit is working on you, you're not going to be comfortable no matter what you're sitting on. And here's the thing, we want the Holy Spirit working on us. Don't we? Maybe the problem is, we don't. It is so much more comfortable to just show up to church, be entertained for a while, be a part of a "positive" conversation and go home. No conviction, no pressure to have to do anything more. Clock in, clock out, check off my Jesus time for the week, I'm good to go! There is a problem, actually there are two problems.

First, as a Christian, if we don't want the Holy Spirit working in our lives (which is impossible since that is His job), we need to stop now and spend some time in prayer, asking God to reveal to us why we are at this point in our life. Literally, put the book down and let's get this settled. 1 Thessalonians 5:19 warns us to "Quench not the Spirit.". One definition of quench is, "extinguish (a fire)". You and I can actually put out the fire that the Holy Spirit is trying to light in us. Remember when you were on fire for God? Maybe you're there now. How do we get back on fire for God or remain on fire for God? First, "Rejoice evermore." (1 Thessalonians 5:16). Let people see how ecstatic you are about God. Everything about who God is and what He does should cause us to live our lives full of joy. Rejoicing stokes the fire and keeps it burning bright. Second, "Pray without ceasing." (1 Thessalonians 5:17). When we desire to live for God, do His will, which according to Romans 12:2 is good, acceptable and perfect, it is important that we talk to the one who put this plan in place for our life before the foundation of the world. That's what praying is. It's just talking to God. I believe God gets excited when His children want to talk to Him and think about what God might do when He is excited. Third, "In every thing give thanks:" (1 Thessalonians 5:18). Ok, do I really need to say anymore on this one other than every thing means EVERY THING! You want to get back in the game or stay strong in the fight? REJOICE…PRAY…GIVE THANKS!

The second problem is more grave. The first work of the Holy Spirit is to convict us of our sin. John 16:8 tells us, "And when he is come, he will reprove the world of sin, and of righteousness, and of judgment.". The "he" spoken of here is the Holy Spirit. If you are not experiencing any conviction from the Holy Spirit and you should be, we all do, then that can only mean one thing. It means you have never been born again into the body of Christ. As a Christian, when we sin, the Holy Spirit convicts us of that sin. We may not respond in the right way, but we know we've sinned because of that conviction. So, if you are not experiencing conviction of sin, then you can't be a child of God. It's that simple and praise God it is that simple. You don't have to guess or question if you are saved. The indwelling of the Holy Spirit is a promise from God for those who receive His Son. "And I will put my spirit within you, and cause you to walk in my statutes, and ye shall keep my judgments, and do them." (Ezekiel 36:27). I know this is the case because it is my story.

I was in 8th grade and our family had just started attending a new church in our area. We hadn't been there long when my brother received Christ as his Savior. I remember the Sunday morning he went forward to share his decision. After the Pastor talked with him for a minute, he invited the whole church to come up and shake my brothers hand. I don't know if the whole church did, but it seemed like it. As someone who was big into playing sports, this struck me. It was like my brother had hit the game winner. Everyone was excited and congratulating him. There was a part of me that wanted some of that. A few weeks later at the end of our Sunday School hour, my teacher said what he usually did each week at the end of class. He said, "If you would like to get saved today, say this prayer.". I thought about my brother and the excitement of all the people. I thought, well who doesn't want to get saved. So, as my teacher prayed, I repeated the prayer. I later went forward in church, just like my brother had and experienced the same "game winner" feeling. Life was good and I thought I was too.

Jump ahead several years. I am now 19 years old and a Freshman in college. The question, "Am I really saved?" had troubled me for a while now, but I just shrugged it off as the devil trying to mess with me and make me doubt. One day, though, I just couldn't get the thought out of my head. I knew it wasn't the devil. I knew God was making it clear to me that the prayer I had said years earlier wasn't one of repentance, but one motivated by self. I took care of things that day with my College and Career class leader. It was later that day that God showed me the difference between the two experiences. I don't remember what it was I did, I really don't, but I remember the feeling of conviction for doing wrong. It was like God was asking me, do you remember how you used to feel about doing that and I thought, it never bothered me before. But now, God asked? Oh, I know it was wrong, please forgive me. He said, that's how you know for sure you are saved. You now have the Holy Spirit inside you. I've never forgotten that. Maybe that is where you are. You've said the prayer or you're trusting in the fact that you go to church or you've been told you just have to love Jesus, but you know you've never truly been born again. Don't wait any longer. This is why Jesus went about the cities and villages. He knew the need of the people, just like He knows your need and He stands ready to forgive your sins, because of what Jesus did on the cross, and welcome you into His family. Spend some time talking with Jesus now. Call out to Him to forgive you of your sins and know that you have eternal life. If you have already accepted Christ as Savior, spend some time rejoicing in your salvation and thanking Him through prayer and ask Him to grow your desire to take the Gospel to the cities and villages.

Here is a reminder of what the Gospel is, what its purpose is and our role in it. What does scripture say the Gospel is? "For I delivered unto you first of all that which I also received, how that **Christ died for our sins** according to the scriptures; And that **he was buried**, and that **he rose again the third day** according to the scriptures:" (1 Corinthians

15:3-4) (Emphasis mine). What does scripture say the purpose of the Gospel is? "For I am not ashamed of the gospel of Christ: for **it is the power of God unto salvation** to every one that believeth; to the Jew first, and also to the Greek." (Romans 1:16) (Emphasis mine). What does scripture say our role in the Gospel is? "And he said unto them, Go ye into all the world, and **preach the gospel to every creature.**" (Mark 16:15) (Emphasis mine). Scripture should be sufficient as our authority concerning the Gospel, but scripture is being questioned today, even by churches, as to whether it is relevant for today. Let me just say, if scripture isn't relevant today, then it has never been relevant. If God never changes, why would His word change? It wouldn't! So, just consider this question about church.

In its services, is your church, through the teaching of scripture, seeking the encouraging and convicting work of the Holy Spirit in your life? Is your church striving to help you grow in your faith for the purpose of accomplishing God's plan for your life, which is to take the Gospel message into the cities and villages He has called you to?

What cities and villages might you walk through this week? A local restaurant or grocery store? Your work or school? The post office or mall? Maybe your doctor's office or where you get your hair cut? Whether it is in your local community or a foreign community, they are all cities and villages where God has commanded you to "go". My prayer is that you will utter the words of the Apostle Paul in Romans 1:15, "So, as much as in me is, I am ready to preach the gospel...". I hope you will make it to your final destination. Last call for flight...!

Pray Through

"Therefore shall not any man be able to stand before thee all the days of thy life: as I was with Moses, so I will be with thee: I will not fail thee, nor forsake thee. Have not I commanded thee? Be strong and of a good courage; be not afraid, neither be thou dismayed: for the Lord thy God is with thee whithersoever thou goest." (Joshua 1:5, 9)

CHAPTER 2

The Busyness of the Aisle

"And Jesus went about all the cities and villages,
teaching in their synagogues,..."
— MATTHEW 9:35 —

Nonstop (except for the takeoff and landing obviously) during the flight, someone is always busy "doing" something. People are constantly moving around. Going to the restroom. Walking around to stretch their legs. Opening the overhead compartment to get something from their bags. Even in their seats people are busy. Working on their computer, playing games on their phones or tablets, or even an old-fashioned game of cards. The flight crew works their way back and forth, up and down the aisle, serving the passengers snacks, drinks, and meals. They attend to the call button for pillows, blankets, earbuds and such. They work to keep the trash cleared so each passenger will be as comfortable as they can in their small area of the plane. Constant movement takes place on these overnight flights. Busyness! In the window seat, you may choose to take an occasional glimpse of all the action, but you can easily remain oblivious to all the busyness surrounding you. But not so in the aisle seat. Oh, no! All of it is right in front of you, vying for your attention, screaming, look at me! Your eyes seem to dart back and forth, trying to capture and decipher all that is taking place. The mother, a couple of rows up, bouncing her little boy up and down as he cries and fusses. The gentleman in the aisle seat next to you who, off and on, continues the conversation started earlier in the flight. Hey, he's trying to take it all in too! The two or three people standing at the bathroom causing you to debate, do I need to use the restroom? Should I go now and wait in line allowing my legs to get a stretch? Maybe I'll wait a few minutes and let the line go down. Here comes the food and drink cart. Tuck your elbow in! Do I want something to drink right now? I guess I will have to wait to go to the bathroom. But, amongst all the chaos, God will simply and quietly whisper in your ear, I love them. I died for them so that they too may have life. So, Tony, you love them too, as I have loved you. God first taught me this lesson during a trip to Australia in the late 1990's.

I had been to Australia twice before. Because of the distance, I had accumulated enough miles to upgrade my seats. But, I only had enough miles to upgrade one way. Looking back now, I'm not sure why, but I chose to do the upgrade going and not coming home. So, from Indianapolis to Denver, Colorado and then from Denver to San Francisco, California, I flew first class. You know, Mr. Scellato, real silverware, better food. Anything you wanted and as much of it as you wanted. Then from San Francisco to Sydney, Australia, I flew upstairs in Business Class. Both of these areas are like the window seat, but to the max! It's quiet. Movement is slow. You are completely unaware and unconcerned about the chaos that is taking place just on the other side of that curtain or down below. But, on the way home, it was quite a different experience. I was back in coach, but not just anywhere in coach. God had arranged a special seat for me. It was the aisle seat right next to the center restrooms. On the larger planes there are bathrooms in the front, center, and rear to accommodate all the people. Now, the center bathrooms are the ones that most of the passengers use (or at least so it seemed).

I learned two specific things during that 13+ hour flight from Sydney back to Los Angeles. One, I believe God does have a sense of humor, as if creating you and me didn't already provide evidence. Two, that through His sense of humor, there are valuable lessons to be learned. Through a conversation I started with the person in the aisle seat across from me (yes, I am now "that guy"), I learned that there was a very large group of High School and College aged students on our flight. They had travelled to Australia as part of an educational program and were now on their way back home to the United States. What I hadn't been told was, they were separated into groups and given sleep shift assignments! Ok, so the sleep shift assignments is just my opinion, but, for the next 13+ hours, it was literally a steady flow of these students making their way back and forth from, that's right, you guessed it, the center bathrooms. And as they stood, congregated right at my seat, some were quite chatty, some still very excited about their experience in Australia, and some extremely slap-happy, maybe because they are teens or maybe because it was getting close to their "shift" to take a nap and get re-energized. Needless to say, any rest or relaxation was brief as the next herd (I love young people, so I like to give them a little razzing) of young people made their way to my location. It was like Times Square in New York City! My seat had become "The city that never sleeps."

We don't read much about Jesus sleeping, though we know He would have. I don't think it's because that would make for boring reading, but because the emphasis we see on Jesus' ministry was that He was always busy ministering to someone, somewhere. Jesus definitely sat in the aisle seat. He wasn't busy doing nothing, either. He was busy with and for a purpose. Our verse tells us that Jesus was busy teaching, preaching and healing. Think about this, too. Jesus' ministry was only considered to be about 3 years in length. That's not a very long time, but look at all that Jesus did. He couldn't have done all of the things we read about in the Bible if He wasn't busy, or as we might say, if He wasn't gettin' after it! But, consider also what scripture tells us. We read and say, man, Jesus did a whole lot in a short period of time, but what we read about wasn't even the half of what He did. John 21:25 tells us, "And there are also many other things which Jesus did, the which, if they should be written every one, I suppose that even the world itself **could not contain** the books that should be written. Amen." (Emphasis mine). Wow! How do you even wrap your brain around that? Jesus had to be non-stop, kind of like that herd of buffalo (I mean group of teens) I mentioned earlier on my flight home from Australia. In fact, we see Jesus continuing even when the others couldn't. Remember right before Jesus was arrested, He and three of His disciples went to the Garden of Gethsemane to pray. Remember what happened? "Then cometh Jesus with them unto a place called Gethsemane, and saith unto the disciples, Sit ye here, while I go and pray yonder. And he took with him Peter and the two sons of Zebedee, and began to be sorrowful and very heavy. Then saith he unto them, My soul is exceeding sorrowful, even unto death: tarry ye here, and watch with me. And he went a little farther, and fell on his face, and prayed, saying, O my Father, if it be possible, let this cup pass from me: nevertheless not as I will, but as thou wilt. And he cometh unto the disciples, and findeth them asleep, and saith unto Peter, What, could you not watch with me one hour?" (Matthew 26:36-40). The scripture goes on to tell us that Jesus went to pray again and when He returned, He found the disciples asleep again. Prayer is a huge part of ministry. It is vital and yet these three disciples couldn't keep up with Jesus. It's hard to stay busy when you are tired, but Jesus shows us it is important to stay busy, even when we are tired. Surely Jesus was tired too, but what was about to take place was more important and needed covered in prayer more than He needed sleep. I don't know about you reading this, but as I write, man, am I feeling convicted. As I said earlier in this book, I struggle with these things too, just like you. In this chapter, we're going to focus on the aspect of teaching. Now, I know as Jesus went about all the cities and villages, He also preached and healed people and those aspects of His ministry were very important as well, so we will touch on those in Chapter 3. What we are taught plays such a large role in the foundation of our life and so I wanted to shed some light, especially on the aspect of spiritual teaching, and what it looks like in today's American church.

Teaching is defined a couple of ways. One definition is, "ideas or principles taught by an authority". A second definition is, "Teaching is the process of attending to people's needs, experiences and feelings, and intervening so that they learn particular things, and go beyond the given". Both of these definitions just scream JESUS! Jesus is the

13

ultimate authority, "For he taught them as one having authority, and not as the scribes." (Matthew 7:29). Jesus attends to our every need, "But my God shall supply all your need according to his riches in glory by Christ Jesus." (Philippians 4:19). Jesus always intercedes on behalf of His children, "Wherefore he is able also to save them to the uttermost that come unto God by him, seeing he ever liveth to make intercession for them." (Hebrews 7:25). Jesus will take us farther than our wildest dreams, "Now unto him that is able to do exceeding abundantly above all that we ask or think, according to the power that worketh in us," (Ephesians 3:20). These are the outcomes when Jesus taught and can also be the outcomes when we teach.

Are we seeing these outcomes in the American church today? I don't know. It seems like a lot of people are excited about Jesus, I see a lot of I Heart Jesus t-shirts, but is that excitement actually resulting in souls being saved? Are people truly understanding their sin and, therefore, turning to the Savior or are they having an emotional experience that leads them to say, "I love Jesus"? I think we have to start by looking at the teaching that is being done, how it is being done and who is the authority behind it. So, let's go to our authority. God's Word tells us, "And the things that thou hast heard of me among many witnesses, the same commit thou to faithful men, who shall be able to teach others also." (2 Timothy 2:2). It's simple, take God's word (the truth of it), be faithful to live it and then teach it to others. Please don't just breeze over the very critical part of that last sentence. We are to live out faithfully the **truth** of God's word. Let's breakdown the points, 1) The teaching that is being done, 2) How it is being done and 3) The authority behind the teaching.

We will actually take these points in reverse order, but before we get into it, we need to understand something of great importance. Please don't miss this. No matter how much teaching we are listening to, in churches, books, online, on television, etc., it is our personal responsibility to study and know why we believe what we believe. I can't just say because my Pastor or some author or speaker says it, it must be true. I am to go study what I am being taught to make sure it is true. Any good teacher of the word will tell you this and will strongly encourage you to do it. Why? Because a good teacher knows the importance of you being in the word. It is how you grow in your faith and how you will grow closer to God. That is what any good teacher wants for their student.

Now, let's hit these points. First, what or who is the authority behind what is being taught throughout the American church today? As Christians, we would say, well God is, right? Right? But, it's not the case. As I will make the case later, what is being taught today in the American church, the "who" is man and the "what" is culture. We, "man", have decided that scripture is no longer culturally relevant or sensitive. It worked two thousand years ago for Jesus, but just doesn't work for us today. Oh, the Bible is still important, but we just need to better understand it as it applies differently to our culture today. I'm sorry folks (not really), but this is where God is "a little" different than we are. "There hath no temptation taken you but such as is common to man: but God is faithful, who will not suffer you to be tempted above that ye are able; but will with the temptation also make a way to escape, that ye may be able to bear it." (1 Corinthians 10:13). Do you know what this means friends? It means Jesus was relevant in Old Testament times, New Testament times, today, and, if God tarries another one million years, Jesus will still be relevant! Do we understand that if we say scripture is not relevant today, we are saying Jesus is not relevant today? Does that really make sense? Who wrote scripture? God did. "For the prophecy came not in old time by the will of man: but holy men of God spake as they were moved by the Holy Ghost." (2 Peter 1:21). "All scripture is given by inspiration of God…" (2 Timothy 3:16). Who is Jesus? Read John 1:1. It says in the beginning, at creation, was the Word, a name given to Jesus. It continues to say the Word, Jesus, was with God and that the one named Word, Jesus, WAS GOD. Maybe you've never been taught that. Don't be surprised, you aren't alone. Scripture makes clear that Jesus is God. So, if scripture is God's word and Jesus is God, then Jesus has never changed and thus Jesus is absolutely relevant today. The **only way** God is not relevant today is if man has taken over the position of authority. So, who is in charge of your life? Is it you or God? It's a fair question and one we should answer if we truly want to have an impact for Jesus. Let's look at the lives of two different families. The first family decided they wanted to be in charge of their own life. The second family decided to trust God being in charge of their life. I'll let you decide which family made the better choice.

The first family is a young couple, newlyweds you might say. They live in paradise and don't have any children yet. Just starting out, they had the decision to make, who would be in control of their life, you know, where they would live, what they would do for a career, how many kids they wanted, all the decisions a young couple makes. Oh yea, the young couples names are Adam and Eve. Their story goes like this.

They were a match made in heaven, literally! They lived in the best neighborhood and Adam's gardening job was the best gig around. His boss (God) put him in charge of everything and even told Adam he could take as much food home for himself and Eve as he wanted, except from the one single tree that belonged to the boss. He said, if you eat from that tree, there will be serious consequences. One tree amongst probably thousands! Of course Adam said, No problem boss! Then, the neighbor shows up. You know the one, always has an opinion, seems to have everything (though he really has nothing) and gives horrible advice. As he and Eve were talking, she mentioned the one tree that she and Adam couldn't eat from. She said the boss told Adam there would be serious consequences if they ate from it, but that it was no big deal to them since there were so many trees they could eat from with so many options of food. Remember, Adam and Eve knew how important they were to the boss, how much He loved them and wanted the absolute best for them. Of course it was a big deal to the bitter neighbor. He first questions Eve's hearing by saying, Did God really say…? Then he takes it a step further by suggesting that the reason the boss (God) doesn't want them to eat of the one tree is because then they will be just like the boss. Then he plants the deadly seed. He looks Eve square in the eye and says, "Wouldn't it be great to be your own boss?" Of course, we know Eve's answer was yes and that she convinced Adam that he could be just as good a boss to lead their family. So, what was the result of Adam and Eve's decision? First, they were evicted from the neighborhood. Adam started his own gardening business, but the only ground he could find was riddled with weeds and was almost impossible to work. Adam and Eve started a family, but their first two sons didn't get along and one ended up murdering the other. And, to show the lasting effect of bad decisions, Adam and Eve's decision to be the authority in their own lives determined how you and I would come into this world…as sinners, "Wherefore, as by one man sin entered into the world, and death by sin; and so death passed upon all men, for that all have sinned:" (Romans 5:12). I think it would be safe to say that Adam and Eve chose the window seat. You can read all about this family in Genesis 2-4.

The second family was quite different. They definitely sat in the aisle seat. They were an older couple with three boys who were grown and married themselves. Noah was 500 years old when God came to him and said, I've got a job for you. God told Noah that he and his family were the only people on earth that pleased Him (God) and that He (God) was going to destroy everyone else who was living. Can you imagine that conversation! Can you imagine the conversation Noah had with his wife and kids? But, there is more to this unbelievable story.

Why was God going to destroy everyone on earth and how was He going to do it? God said that everyone on earth, apart from Noah's family, was wicked all day, every day. So, He told Noah to build a big boat because it was going to rain big time! Now, you may think, if you don't know the account, what's the big deal. Well, first, it was going to rain so much that the whole world would flood. Second, the boat Noah was to build would be 450 feet long (equal to one and a half football fields), 75 feet wide and 45 feet tall (that is a three-story plus building). But, there is more. Since Noah and his family were on the aisle, that means things wouldn't be easy. As Noah and his sons built the ark, which took around 120 years, 120 YEARS, they were telling the people that God was going to judge the world through rain and they needed to get into the boat in order to be saved. For 100 years, the people mocked Noah and his sons, even the men they hired to help build the ark probably mocked them. Why? Because there message was an impossibility. Remember, before the flood, water came from the ground. There was no such thing as rain! God had yet to open the firmament. And, if you just wanted to go fishing, do you really need that big of a boat? Stop and think about it. How would you have responded? How do you respond now when God is asking you to do the impossible? For 120 years, Noah was faithful to proclaim the message God told him to proclaim to the people. He did so, because he wasn't in charge of his life. God was the authority in Noah's life. Genesis 7:1 says, "And the Lord said unto Noah, Come thou and all thy house into the ark; for thee have I seen righteous before me in this generation." At 600 years old, Noah and his wife, his sons and their wives, entered the ark and God shut the door. I can tell you, when God shuts the door of one's heart, that is it. It's over! The rain began to fall and the people perished. Read the account of Noah in Genesis 6-9.

We will look at the next two questions together, what is being taught today and how it is being taught. I believe what you will find is that the position of authority is at the foundation of what is being taught. I believe many "leaders" in the American church have decided to take the authority role in their "ministries". This isn't anything new, though. Since the fall in the garden, man has tried to make his own way in the world, be his own Master. We see a move to soften and actually change the Gospel message so that the cross is more palatable and Jesus is more acceptable to a wayward generation. I challenge anyone to do an in depth study of what Jesus went through before and during His crucifixion. The brutality of it is unimaginable. He did all of that because of our sin. He endured all of that brutality because He loves you and me. Jesus was taken to a point of being unrecognizable so that we may recognize Him as our Savior. Nothing about what Christ did was soft or palatable. It was horrific and awesome and it is part of the Gospel message (death, burial, and resurrection) that scripture says has the power to save (see Romans 1:16). As faithful followers of Jesus, we need to be ready to stand boldly against the evil spirit of this age and proclaim the absolute truth of the Gospel. Why would anyone want to change that message? Because doing so changes who is in the position of authority. It all started with Lucifer. He wanted to be God. He so deceived himself that he actually tried to tempt Jesus (God the Son). We saw it with Adam and Eve. Their decision is still negatively impacting people today (sin). We saw it with the Pharisees and other religious leaders. Jesus referred to them as a den of vipers for deceiving the people to think their works was what would save them. And, we see it today, just as in Jesus' time, through false teachers. These men (and women) claim to teach the truth of the word, but fail to teach the whole truth. I have no issue comparing these people to Satan, who used scripture, twisting it a little for his own purpose. You may be saying, wow, Tony, that is harsh. Aren't you being judgmental? No, I'm not. I'm warning based on what Jesus said. In Matthew 7:15, it states, "Beware of false prophets, which come to you in sheep's clothing, but inwardly they are *ravening* wolves." (Emphasis mine). Acts 20:29 says, "For I know this, that after my departing shall grievous wolves enter in among you, *not sparing* the flock." (Emphasis mine). Friends, we cannot turn a blind eye to this. Quit supporting these wolves on TV (not everyone on TV is bad) with your money. Stop supporting these wolves by buying their books (hopefully not everyone who writes a book is a wolf). And, even more so, quit supporting these wolves in the church you attend (if they fit the description Jesus gave of what a wolf looks like). You need to be able to discern the source of your leader's authority. Is it from their own perceived wisdom or is it from the Word of God? If the individual Christian spends time studying and learning God's Word, it will be easy to discern the source of their authority by their teaching. Ask, "Is this the speaker's opinion or is it the Word of God?" We need to pray for our leaders to stay strong in teaching the whole truth of scripture. We should pray for conviction leading those who lean on their own understanding to repent and return to teaching truth, yielding to God's rightful authority – before He shuts the door of the boat.

So, what is being taught today in many American churches that is of concern and what do we do about it? We may touch on specific topics, but I want to introduce 3 belief systems which under most of today's false teachings fall. These three beliefs are 1) Universalism, 2)

New Age Movement and 3) The Emerging Church. Let's look at what each of these beliefs teach and how, as Christians, you and I should respond to those who teach them.

Universalism teaches that all paths lead to God and eternal life and so all people will ultimately be saved. A popular example of this teaching would be those that claim Christians and Muslims worship the same God. The issue with this particular example is that these two groups view Jesus, who He is, quite differently. The overall issue with the Universalist teaching is man's questioning of God. Specifically, if God is willing to send a person to hell and therefore the need for man to take the position of authority in this matter. Maybe you've heard it taught that God is a God of love (TRUTH), so He would never condemn a person to hell (HALF TRUTH = FALSE). God is a God of love, "For God so loved the world..." (John 3:16). As Christians, we all know and are so thankful for His love. However, God does not condemn a person, but, according to scripture, we condemn ourselves because of the sin we are born with (the continuing effect of Adam's decision) that causes us to not believe in Jesus. John 3:17-19 says, "For God sent **not** his Son into the world to condemn the world; but that the world through him might be saved. He that believeth on him is not condemned: but he that believeth not is condemned already, because he hath not believed in the name of the only begotten Son of God. And this is the condemnation, that light is come into the world, and men loved darkness rather than light, because their deeds were evil." (Emphasis mine). Ok, I see what scripture says, but God is so much about His love, He wouldn't actually send someone to hell, would He? "Then shall he say also unto them on the left hand, Depart from me, ye cursed, into everlasting fire, prepared for the devil and his angels. And these shall go away into everlasting punishment." (Matthew 25:41, 46). Do you see the need to know the truth of scripture? It is quite important that you do. Sure, it sounds good to tell people the Universalist view, that God loves everybody and so everyone is "ok", but for the sake of their eternity, it is vital, it is necessary, that a person knows the truth of what scripture says.

How do we respond then to the Universalist teaching? In love, but with bold conviction, we speak the truth. The only way a person can be saved is through Jesus Christ. A person must repent and in faith, call on the name of Jesus to receive eternal life.

Read: Acts 4:12, Matthew 25:46, Hebrews 9:27, Romans 10:9, 10, 13

Memorize: "Jesus saith unto him, I am the way, the truth, and the life: no man cometh unto the Father, but by me." (John 14:6)

The New Age Movement teaches a belief system of Eastern influence that emphasizes universal tolerance and moral relativism. Moral relativism says you do what feels good to you, that man himself is divine and can create his own reality and identity. You can quickly see the allure of this teaching. Though it has had a resurgence in popularity within the American church, it's not a new teaching. We see it all throughout scripture where man decides his pleasure is more important than doing what pleases God.

Remember Adam and Eve? God said you can eat everything, but the fruit off of this one tree. Then the serpent comes in and, of course, points out the yumminess of that tree and tells Eve that God just doesn't want her and Adam to have any fun, know anything important, be anything in life. He "encourages" Eve to enjoy life, do what makes you feel good, what pleases you and, by the way, God will be ok with it because He loves you. Eve's response to the serpent's pitch was, "And when the woman saw that the tree was **good** for food, and that it was **pleasant** to the eyes, and a tree to be **desired** to make one wise, she took of the fruit thereof, and did eat, and gave also unto her husband with her, and he did eat." (Genesis 3:6) (Emphasis mine). SHE ATE IT! SHE PROCLAIMED, I AM SOVEREIGN (possessing supreme or ultimate power). Again, moral relativism, a tenet of the New Age teaching, makes the claim that man himself is divine. This was the allure that caused Eve to "bite". This is the same allure that has made many in the American church bite today. The push to be "culturally relevant" has caused many church "leaders" to begin to teach the acceptance of things such as alcohol use and the homosexual lifestyle. Now, this is just my opinion, so I encourage you to look up some of today's prominent church "leaders" and find out for yourself where they stand on topics like these and what they teach about them.

My opinion is they are suggesting Christians need to rethink their beliefs in the Bible. Rethink God's word! Why? Why would you need to rethink what God has said? The only answer is because you desire to be the Divine and have a position of authority that overrides the authority of God's Word.

In the days of Noah, you could say this teaching was being lived out big time. I mean big time! "And God saw that the wickedness of man was great in the earth, and that every imagination of the thoughts of his heart was only evil continually. And it repented the Lord that he had **made** man on the earth, and it grieved him at his heart. And the Lord said, I will destroy man whom I have **created** from the face of the earth; both man, and beast, and the creeping thing, and the fowls of the air; for it repenteth me that I have **made** them." (Genesis 6:5-7) (Emphasis mine). Population estimates put 750 million to 4 billion people living on earth at this time and yet God only spared eight (Noah, his wife, their three boys and their wives.). What was the moral relativism issue going on here? The issue is, God created everything, but man was living as if he could create his own reality and identity. People were worshipping the creature (themselves) instead of the Creator (God) as it tells us in Romans chapter one. How do we see that played out today? A couple ways immediately come to mind. Have you noticed how we will fight to "Save the Turtles" or some other animal, yet, at the writing of this book, since 1973 over 61 million babies have been killed through abortion with very little resistance from the church. The other is the frenzy over global warming and the worry that the world will come to an end within the next decade or so because of it. I'm just going to leave it at this, go read from Genesis 1 to Revelation 22 and I think what you will find is that nothing is going to happen to the earth until God says it is over. A couple other verses I recommend you look up to reaffirm this idea that man wanted to do what he wanted to do are, Judges 17:6 and Proverbs 21:2.

How do we respond to the New Age teaching? In love, but with bold conviction, we speak the truth. It's simple, we stand on the truth that there is only one sovereign God and Creator of all things.

Read: Isaiah 55:8-9 and Hebrews 2:5-10

Memorize: "In whose hand is the soul of every living thing, and the breath of all mankind." (Job 12:10)

The Emerging Church movement is one that focuses its message of the gospel through culturally sensitive methods. "Leaders" of this movement teach Jesus' life as an allegory or narrative and not as a true event. The movement is very inclusive of several belief systems and puts an emphasis on emotion versus absolute truth. Because of that, they teach there is no hell, no judgment and no need of forgiveness. They glorify honesty and confession, but without repentance. This softening of the gospel and downplaying who Jesus truly is, sets a strong foundation for man being the ultimate authority in his own life. The teaching that scripture is not infallible and changes with the times, as the Emergent movement and these other false belief systems teach, sadly leads many trusting people astray and leaves them without a true hope. The totally disgusting aspect of this is these false teachers, in the name of Christianity, are actually leading people away from Christ and towards an eternal hell (which these teachers say doesn't exist). If you are a true follower of Jesus, this ought to both tick you off and also drive you to your knees in prayer. Why? I challenge you to go study how God deals with people who decide they don't need Him. It's never pretty, but it is always just.

How do we respond to the Emergent Movement teaching? In love, but with bold conviction, we speak the truth. If we soften or water down the Gospel message then we do not have good news to share with people.

Read: Galatians 1:8-9, 1 Corinthians 15:1-4 and Exodus 20:3-6

Memorize: "I said therefore unto you, that ye shall die in your sins: for if ye believe not that I am he, ye shall die in your sins." (John 8:24) (this death refers to an eternal death)

Jesus Christ is the only one that can free us from sin and conform us to His image.

Read: 1 John 5:3-5, Philippians 3:7-9 and Galatians 5:16

The busyness of the aisle is hard work, but worthwhile work. Sure, you could sit in the comfort of the window seat and just go with whatever you are taught, but consider what the consequences may be.

You may have friends that never truly see their need of a Savior. For that matter, you may never fully understand your need of a Savior. So, sit in the aisle seat. Get busy! Arm yourself with the Word of God so that you know it and can reinforce biblical doctrine and then always speak the truth in love. Keep God and the word He has given you, your highest authority. "In whom the god of this world hath blinded the minds of them which believe not, lest the light of the glorious gospel of Christ, who is the image of God, should shine unto them. For we preach not ourselves, but Christ Jesus the Lord;" (2 Corinthians 4:4-5).

Pray Through

"So then faith cometh by hearing, and hearing by the word of God." (Romans 10:17)

CHAPTER 3

Watching the Clouds Go By

**"... and preaching the gospel of the kingdom, and healing
every sickness and every disease among the people."**
— MATTHEW 9:35 —

Peter, having made this flight many times, was kind enough to allow me to sit in the window seat, giving me the opportunity to see some of Paris, though it was still early morning when we arrived, and the night lights of Mumbai as we came in for landing. "Crew, prepare cabin for landing", the pilot spoke over the intercom. A long flight almost finished. A friendly voice came over the intercom. It was the flight crew leader. She said, "Ladies and gentlemen, welcome to Mumbai, India. Local time is 11:30 p.m.". It is now Friday, October 3rd.

What I hadn't given much thought to was how much time I had spent from Chicago to Mumbai just gazing out the window. As we took off and ascended above the clouds, I would stare at them for hours. Then as we would make our descent to land, I just peering out at the fields, the streets and highways, the farm areas and cities below, which seemed so distant and small. I was simply "doing my own thing" and unaware of the need that I was gazing upon. I couldn't see it. It wasn't in front of me. Though it surely was there, to me, no thought that it even existed. It's just like flying high above the clouds. The ground is below, but you can't see it. All you see are clouds. You just watch as each cloud goes by. Oh, maybe you see them as another object for a moment, but then they simply vanish away. For hours, watching the clouds go by, caught up in it, with no thought of involving yourself in what is happening just feet away.

After landing, we retrieved our bags, made our way through customs, and headed out to meet Peter's cousins, who had come to pick us up and take us to their apartment to clean up, eat, and rest. We would catch a flight to Hyderabad, our first ministry stop, later that evening. By now it is past midnight and Saturday, October 4th.

As we made our way through the streets of Mumbai, a city of 22 million people, I caught glimpses of the crowds still mingling about the streets, though it was nearing 1:00 a.m. But, my mind was more focused on how tired my body felt. As Peter would point out things for me to see, I would take a brief glance, give a nod of the head or maybe a quiet yes, but, as it was in the plane, the people passed by and quickly vanished away in the night, just as the clouds did. I gave them about as much thought as I had the clouds. I can tell you, the challenge put forth in this book is the same challenge God puts to me often. It is an area of my Christian walk where I have struggles too. The hustle and bustle of life keeps us so busy, busy doing good things often, but so busy that we can't or don't even see the need that is all around us. We are doing good things, but that doesn't mean we're doing the right things. I believe that is the point Jesus is making in verse 35. Let me explain.

What is your ministry, the calling God has given you? Are you an IT guy like my friend Peter? Maybe you are a farmer, a doctor, a plumber or a child life specialist? Have you been called to be a Pastor, a missionary to a foreign land, a housewife, an author? You get my point. Wherever God has placed you is your ministry. Don't get caught up thinking that ministry is only something your Pastor is supposed to do. If you are a Christian, a follower of Jesus Christ, you are in ministry. This thought may blow some of your minds because you've always thought ministry was for the pastors only. Now that we have established you can be a Christian accountant, social worker or electrician, the next question is, where is your ministry? Do you see it as merely contained within the four walls of your work, so to speak? Is it just at the office? Is it just at church? Is it just at home? Though your ministry definitely happens in those places, it is far more reaching than that. Consider the impact your ministry has on those around you in your workplace, but then consider how much greater the impact of your ministry could be if you didn't keep it inside the "box" of where you work. What could or would happen if you allowed God to expand our ministry? It is actually what we are supposed to do, at least according to the example that Jesus sets.

Our text for this chapter says that, *"…and preaching the gospel of the kingdom, and healing every sickness and every disease among the people."* See, Jesus was a teacher, preacher and healer, but he didn't just do these things at His office in Nazareth. No, He took these gifts and many others to where the people were. He took His ministry to the streets! Jesus' ministry was spent showing and living this example in front of people and especially in front of His disciples. Then at the end of Jesus' ministry, after He had gone to the cross and arose from the dead, He reminds His disciples of this example they are to live out. Just before He ascended back to heaven, Jesus told His disciple, "Go ye therefore, and teach all nations, baptizing them in the name of the Father, and of the Son, and of the Holy Ghost: Teaching them to observe all things whatsoever I have commanded you: and, lo, I am with you always, even unto the end of the world. Amen." (Matthew 28:19-20). This was to be part of their everyday life, wherever they might go and wherever they did go. Oh, and before we just write this off as a conversation only meant for a time long ago, let's be clear about this scripture. It is the same command that God has given to us today. You know, some things are timeless! God's word is one of those things. Just as then, we are to be about the Gospel message in every aspect and part of our day.

My guess is, if we really look at how most of our days go, they aren't just spent inside the "box". Maybe your morning starts at the gym. Maybe you grab a quick breakfast at McDonalds or a coffee from Dunkin Donuts (sorry, I'm not a big fan of Starbucks!). These are all people you see when you sit in the aisle seat. What about during your day? Does it consist of outside meetings, lunch dates, trips to the grocery store or the mall? More people roaming the aisle. Do you travel for your work? Airports, hotels, restaurants are all full of lost souls if we will notice them. What about after work? We attend our kids' ballgames, play on a softball team, dinner with friends, all kinds of things. And, yet we think our ministry only takes place inside the "box" from 8:00 a.m. to 5:00 p.m. I dare to say, if we only look for opportunities for ministry inside the "box", we miss the largest part of our ministry chances during the day, those in the cities and villages we pass through.

These opportunities outside our ministry "box" are not always easy. In fact, they are probably more difficult. We don't know these people as well. There are often more consequences for our sharing the Gospel message. We are often in the fight alone, or at least it seems we are alone. The great news is, we are never alone, "...for he hath said, I will never leave thee, nor forsake thee." (Hebrews 13:5). The greater news is that your ministry, my ministry, isn't about us. It is all about Jesus and since it is about Him, He takes care of the details. He knows the beginning and the end and everything in between. He gives us the strength to do the ministry, the wisdom and words we need. God only asks us to trust and obey Him and leave the results up to Him. The results, His perfect will, are His and His alone. As scripture tells us, some plant, some water, but the increase (the harvest) belong to God (See 1 Corinthians 3:6-7). When Jesus gave the disciples His command in Matthew 28:19-20, He also gave them the hope that they could do what He wanted them to. In Matthew 28:18, Jesus told the disciples, "... All power is given unto me in heaven and in earth." This is awesome news! So often when God is leading us to a ministry opportunity, we start our thoughts (and words) with, "I don't know", "I can't", "What if" or "I'm not sure". Why do we do this? We do this because we believe whatever it is that God wants us to do, we have to accomplish in our own strength, our own power. According to Matthew 28:18, though, we don't have any power (apart from Christ at least). Maybe that is why we stress so much over our Gospel job. Instead of stressing, however, we ought to be excited over the work God gives us. Why? It's simple! Because He has all the power needed to complete the job. It's His job after all. He is the boss we are just the workers. God has promised to give us the tools and knowledge we need for the job and if we get stuck on something, He says all we need to do is ask Him for help and He will give it to us (Stop and read Matthew 7:7-8, Luke 11:9-10, John 15:7, 16, 16:23 and James 1:5). So, as you are sitting reading this and God is saying this is the job I have for you or as you go about your day tomorrow and God says, I have a quick job for you to do, first, thank God for entrusting this job to you and then second, promise God you will faithfully do the job He has asked you to do through His power and strength.

In the last chapter, we looked at the aspect of Jesus teaching as He went about His travels from city to city and village to village. Since we realize that false teachings, which we have examined, have dramatically impacted the American church today, we understand the importance of God's command for us to teach the truth of His Word as we travel through the cities and villages of our life. In this chapter, we will look a little more at the two other areas of Jesus' ministry, preaching and healing, and how we are to incorporate those aspects of ministry into our everyday Gospel ministry as well. These two areas of ministry most definitely require you be seated on the aisle, right in the midst of the battle. Don't get caught staring out at the clouds or else you will miss some absolutely amazing opportunities to see God in all His wonder and glory!

There are a few definitions for the word "preach". One is, "deliver a sermon or religious address to an assembled group of people". Another is, "publicly proclaim or teach (a religious message or belief)". The last one is, "earnestly advocate (a belief or course of action)".

We could look at many famous sermons from some old time preachers like Spurgeon or Moody, but I want to look at one of the first unbelievably amazing sermons in the early days of the church. It was preached by a man named Peter. You remember Peter! He's the disciple that always had something to say and it usually resulted in him putting his foot square in his mouth. His most famous episode came just before Jesus would be crucified. Jesus tells His disciples that they will deny Him and Peter quickly, and very proudly, jumps in and says oh no, no, no Jesus, I'll never deny you, I would die for you before I would deny you. Jesus goes on to tell Peter that not only will he deny

Jesus, but he will deny Him three times. I can just see the expression and almost look of disgust on Peter's face when Jesus said that. Shaking his head (the way I picture it), Peter says no way Jesus will I do that. Well, you know the rest of the story, Peter denied knowing Jesus three times and then the rooster crowed.

That, however, was the proud Peter. But, what happened when Peter repented of that sin and began living his ministry in the power of Christ. Jesus was crucified and resurrected and has now ascended back to heaven. As Jesus had promised, the Holy Spirit (the third person of the Trinity) came after His departure. That descent of the Holy Spirit, in the New Testament, on the Apostles and other disciples was what was being commemorated at the time of the formation of the church and Peter's great sermon. This commemoration is known as Pentecost.

In Acts 2, we see the filling of the Holy Spirit and Peter begins to explain Pentecost to the people. I love how Peter no longer just spouts his opinion, but in his explanation to the people, he quotes the words of both the prophet Joel and of King David. This would and should have held a lot of weight with the people. These would be men they were taught about and would have been familiar with their teachings and writings concerning the coming Messiah. Peter begins his sermon with a little background, some history.

Peter then goes on in his sermon to share more about David and how he and Jesus are connected. He first reminds the people that David is dead and buried (See Acts 2:29) and then of the promise of God to David that the Christ, the Messiah, would come from his lineage. "Therefore being a prophet, and knowing that God had sworn an oath to him, that of the fruit of his loins, according to the flesh, he would raise up Christ to sit on his throne;" (Acts 2:30). David and the Messiah would be related. God swore this to David and we know God cannot and will not break His promises. On a bit of a side note, how cool must that have been for the little shepherd boy turned king to have that promised to him.

Peter goes on to explain in verse 31 of Acts 2, that unlike David, whose body is still in the grave, this Christ that would come from David's lineage (See Matthew 1:1-17) will be resurrected. It says His "soul was not left in hell" (Sheol meaning grave) and that His body would not rot or "see corruption".

Then Peter lowers the boom. I love this part of any sermon. This is the so here's what you need to know part of the message. This is the part that ties the rest of the sermon together and demands a response. Peter had already told them earlier (See Acts 2:22-24) in his sermon who Jesus was and that they were the ones who killed him and now he drives that point home. "This Jesus hath God raised up, whereof we all are witnesses," (vs. 32). He says, you can't hide from it boys, you saw Jesus alive after He was crucified and buried and then with the boldness that God had created in Peter, but now being used the correct way, he tells them, "Therefore let all the house of Israel know assuredly, that God hath made that same Jesus, whom ye have crucified, both Lord and Christ." (vs. 36). Oh, don't miss this! God put a boldness in Peter to speak the truth and God has put that same boldness in you and me. It doesn't take boldness to soften the Gospel, it takes boldness to proclaim it. Peter says, "know assuredly", understand this completely. What? That you (and us), because of our sin, crucified Jesus and that God made Jesus "both Lord and Christ". Jesus is the Messiah, the Savior. I think Peter was speaking the bold and powerful words of Jesus Himself when He told Thomas, "...I am the way, the truth, and the life: no man cometh unto the Father, but by me." (John 14:6).

Peter didn't have to give an altar call. He didn't have to beg people to come follow Jesus. Remember what I said earlier about this ministry stuff being about Jesus, not us? Jesus says, here's the job I want you to do (preach to these people) and I will give you the tools you need (boldness) and the words to say (the Gospel message) and I'll take care of the rest. It says, "Now when they heard this, they were pricked in their heart, and said unto Peter and to the rest of the apostles, Men and brethren, *what shall we do?* (vs. 37) (Emphasis mine). As my Pastor would say, Yee Haw! Are you kidding me! Peter just obeyed what God told him to do and He took care of the rest. We saw this same response when Saul, later Paul, was converted on the Damascus Road (See Acts 9:6) and when the Philippian jailor was converted while

Paul and Silas were imprisoned (See Acts 16:30). One last, but very important thing to point out about verse 37 is, this is the fulfillment of the Messianic prophecy made in John 16:8. Peter's humble obedience led to a prophecy being fulfilled. That is a seriously cool thing!

So, what do you do when someone responds to your message with, "So, what do I do?"? Hello! You tell them! You know what to tell them, right? Well, if you're not sure, just listen to Peter's response, "Then Peter said unto them, Repent, and be baptized every one of you in the name of Jesus Christ for the remission of sins, and ye shall receive the gift of the Holy Ghost." (vs. 38). The key to salvation begins with repentance. To repent simply means to turn and go the other direction. In this case, it is turning from a lifestyle of sin and beginning to live a life for Christ. I know longer want to live for myself and the things I desire, but now I desire to live for Jesus and do the things that please Him. It is faith in Jesus Christ that allows us to make this turn and follow Him. Salvation is by faith alone, in Christ alone (Stop and read Ephesians 2:8-9 and John 14:6). I want to make this point because some will read verse 38 and say that one has to both repent and be baptized in order to be saved. But, I just made claim that salvation is by faith alone, nothing else required. So, am I wrong, does scripture contradict itself? What do we do with this? This goes back to proper teaching. If you read further in Acts 3:19, it tells us, "Repent ye therefore, and be converted, that your sins may be blotted out,". It doesn't tell us to do anything else but to repent in order to be "converted" or saved. If you read in Romans, we are told it is as simple as calling out to God to save us. Romans 10:9, 13 say, "That if thou shalt confess with thy mouth the Lord Jesus, and shalt believe in thine heart that God hath raised him from the dead, thou shalt be saved. For whosoever shall call upon the name of the Lord shall be saved.". And, of course, there is probably the most well-known scripture of all time, John 3:16, which tells us eternal life comes from believing in Jesus. Now, I know many great, God loving people that still differ on some of these doctrinal areas, but, what is important is that we look at the entirety of scripture and not just pick one or two verses that we can make fit our point of view. As my brother-in-law and I often talk about, when we get to heaven, I'm sure we are all going to find out where we were right and where we were wrong. But, we also end most every one of our talks with this thought, people sure do need Jesus. Living our lives making sure Jesus is known to those around us can never be wrong.

Peter blew it, then quit, but finally got back up off the mat and decided, people sure do need Jesus! And, so, this day at Pentecost, Peter made sure that these people knew they needed Jesus. I'm sure Peter trusted God for the outcome, but would he have ever imagined what that outcome was going to look like. Repent, Peter told them and repent they did! "Then they that gladly received his word were baptized: and the same day there were added unto them about three thousand souls." (vs. 41). 3,000 people were saved! 3,000!!! I would say that is a Preachers dream. But, that, my friend is the power that God unleashes through obedience. The result is not always in a number, though. Sometimes God's power is shown in how we live our lives. As you finish chapter two of Acts, you see that these three thousand along with the rest of the church are described as continuing together in what they were being taught. They believed together. They cared for each other, together. They worshipped together, fellowshipped together, and praised God together. I believe the power of God is on its greatest display when Christians are together.

The section heading in my bible says, **Faith Prays for the Afflicted**. James 5:13-16 says, "Is any among you afflicted? Let him pray. Is any merry? Let him sing psalms. Is any sick among you? Let him call for the elders of the church; and let them pray over him, anointing him with oil in the name of the Lord: And the prayer of faith shall save the sick, and the Lord shall raise him up; and if he have committed sins, they shall be forgiven him. Confess your faults one to another, and pray one for another, that ye may be healed. The effectual fervent prayer of a righteous man availeth much."

Healing played an important part of Jesus' ministry. It was the proof that He was the Son of God as He claimed. Peter reminded the people of that in his sermon at Pentecost. "Ye men of Israel, hear these words; Jesus of Nazareth, a man approved of God among you by miracles and wonders and signs, which God did by him in the midst of you, as ye yourselves also know:" (Acts 2:22). Jesus gave His disciples the power (through faith) to also heal people at times, but James gives us an idea of how healing is to be a part of our daily ministry today. How can we see people healed today? It can only happen through faithful prayer. Though our text in Matthew talks about Jesus healing sickness and disease, let us not lose sight that, in the middle of all of that, the greatest healing that Jesus was doing, was spiritual healing. Many times, adding to the frustration of the "religious" leaders, when Jesus would heal someone physically, He would tell them their sins had been forgiven. Why would Jesus say that? The people would come to Jesus, in faith, believing who He said He was and therefore knowing He could heal them physically. Not only did many walk away, some literally, healed of a physical impairment or sickness, but also healed of an eternal sickness and given eternal life. I want to share with you one such story of spiritual healing that I was blessed to witness firsthand.

It was December 31, 2012 and we were on the island of Grenada. This was our second team mission trip that we had run through our ministry, YES Ministries. I love doing these trips because you just don't know where God is going to take things and how He is going to use the different team members in His plan. It is so cool to watch how things unfold. This day would definitely go down as one of my top coolest things I've been a part of in ministry.

We started this day with a children's program at Happy Hill Baptist Church in, you guessed it, Happy Hill. Our team loved sharing the Gospel message with the kids through skits and lessons and the love they poured out on these kids I know had to bring a smile to God's face. After our time in Happy Hill, we headed back into the capital city of St. George's for some lunch and then we were going to hand out copies of John and Romans in the streets. With it being New Year's Eve day, coupled with a cruise ship that had come in that morning, the streets were packed with people, both locals and tourists. We brought one thousand copies of the John and Romans and within one hour, they were gone. Most people would take one and move on, but we did get the opportunity to stop and speak with some folks, but you just have to trust that God will take His word and speak to the hearts of people. He did just that in one of the coolest ways I have ever experienced. As we were finishing passing out the copies of John & Romans, I noticed my wife talking to a lady who was with a guy who had a camera. Now, not just any camera, but what looked like a television news cameraman. That is exactly what it was. As I approached them, I heard my wife tell the lady that she needed to talk to me. The lady, who was from the local news station turned to me and asked if she could ask me some questions about our group? They were doing a report for that evening's news about Old Years Night and I guess we looked like a good topic for it. She asked my name, a little about our ministry, and what we were doing on the island. She then turned to our time in the Capital that day and what it was we were handing out. As I began to share about the John & Romans we were passing out, she kept asking me questions about it and why it was important that we handed them out?. It was at that moment, I felt the Holy Spirit prodding me to share the Gospel. My first thought was, "There is no way I'm going to be able to talk about Jesus on TV." But, I jumped right in and figured when she gave the cameraman the sign to "cut it off", well, then I'd be done. I told her how we are all sinners and that our sin separates us from God (and will for all eternity in hell). Camera was still rolling! I continued to share about how Jesus died for our sins because of His great love for us. Still rolling! Now I'm really feeling it! I told her that our message to the folks of Grenada (and the visitors from around the world) was simply that Jesus would save them if they would confess their sin and believe in their heart that Jesus died and rose again for their sin. I couldn't believe it! The camera never stopped! She thanked us for our time and off they went. I never got to see the footage, but many of the church members from the different churches we worked with, came up to me later in our trip and told me how they saw me on the news. How cool is God? I've had the opportunity to share the Gospel in different ways, but never on the local news. This one I'll remember for sure!

As we were pulling out of St. George's, heading back to the hotel for a short rest, Pastor Denis Celestine, one of our host Pastors, said to me, "Please pray brother." I said, "Sure, what's going on?" He proceeded to tell me that they were calling for rain that night. Later that evening, we were going to an area called River Road to put on another children's program, followed by our Old Year's Night (their way of saying New Year's Eve) service. The issue was that where we would be holding these services was outside. Pastor Celestine continued to explain that when it rained, Grenadians run for cover because the rain makes it feel cold outside. I thought, oh man, if no one comes to the service, the night will be ruined. So, I told him absolutely and asked the team to be praying that God would hold the rain off. You can probably see where this is heading.

We arrived at River Road and along with the folks from some of the local churches, we began to set things up for that night. We had worked in this area on a previous trip and used a concrete foundation of a church that had been blown away in a hurricane and had not been rebuilt. Because of the forecast for rain and the fact that we had some musical instruments and sound equipment, we were able to get one of those pop-up canopies for a little cover, not that we were going to need it. After all, we were praying for no rain. We had another great time with the kids that turned out and now it was on to our Old Year's Night service.

We started with some music and, man, I love how the islanders worship the Lord through music. It is so encouraging and contagious! As we sang, people began to trickle in, but not too close. Some of the younger people and maybe their moms would come in, but most of the guys and couples would stand out by or on the road as if that gave them some protection from what was being sung and preached. I will say this, however, most would at least stay and listen even if they wouldn't come in close. One couple stood out to me as soon as they pulled up. It was a man named Alphaeus and his girlfriend, who unfortunately I never learned her name or have forgotten it (which is a possibility with my memory). They pulled up on a motorcycle and, like many others, stayed out by the road. I didn't think about it at the time, but God was already working on both of them. With the skies looking as if they would open up at any moment, why they would have stopped and not hurried to get home, didn't make any sense except that God said "stop". The only thing I can imagine more uncomfortable than running home in a rainstorm is riding a motorcycle on wet, slick roads while getting pelted by the rain. But, there they stood, next to the motorcycle, listening to our service.

My friend Don so graciously accepted the task of preaching the message for our Old Year's Night service. At the time, this was something new for him, at least as far as speaking in a foreign country, but his heart for teaching and just all out love for Jesus and people made me believe he was the perfect guy for this moment. Standing just under the canopy, behind a small pulpit, Don began preaching his message, with several people sitting on the concrete platform and many others standing at a "safe" distance. Soon after Don started, guess what happened? Yep, you guessed it, it started to rain. Pastor Celestine was right, the Grenadians started to scurry for cover and where was the nearest spot to stay dry? Under the canopy! Now all of those standing at their "safe" distance, including Alphaeus and his girlfriend, were right in the "Jesus zone", the one place they tried to avoid. It was awesome! It got a little chaotic as probably forty plus people crammed under our canopy, but Don just kept preaching, seemingly undeterred. The funny thing was that no one thought to have Don turn around since all but two people, who sat under an umbrella on the platform, were now standing behind him. Don would preach and occasionally look over his right shoulder and then his left. It couldn't have been easy, but Don made it look like it was. Oh, and by the way, our prayers concerning the weather were not answered. God saw our hearts and fulfilled our desires to see souls saved – but brought rain. It is an amazing experience when God shows you that His plans are not thwarted by the smallness of our vision. God used the very rain which we dreaded to bring Alphaeus and his girlfriend close. The rain was his tool. We just didn't know it. God's thoughts are truly far above our own and His ways are past our knowing. We just stand in awe and say "Thank you, Lord, for being You."

After Don was done with his message, several men set up a small screen and we began to watch a movie that depicted a young man who died and went to hell. The amazing thing is how the young man died. After yelling at a preacher about how he didn't need God, he and his friend took off on their motorcycles. The young man was goofing off, weaving in and out and then you hear this loud screech and the next thing you see is this guy's bike wrapped around a tree and his body lying there with his head a few feet away. It was graphic for sure, especially for a movie that was filmed by a church in the 60's or 70's. The next frame was this young man screaming in torment in hell. I thought of Alphaeus and wondered how the film was impacting him (what his take on it was) since he was riding his motorcycle that night. After the movie, Pastor Celestine passionately shared with everyone there the truth and reality of hell and how they could know for sure they wouldn't go there. He shared how Christ died for them, was buried, and rose again the third day (the Gospel) and that they could put their faith in that and be saved. The offer was made and then it happened.

Alphaeus came up, but didn't really say anything. Don and I were standing there, so we struck up a conversation with Alphaeus, asking him if he wanted to accept Christ. For what seemed like an hour, but was probably only about 5-10 minutes, we would ask him, "Why did you come forward?", "How can we help you?", "Are you wanting to ask Jesus to save you?" He stood there with his head bowed the whole time and occasionally he would utter something very quietly. It was so faint, that neither Don nor I could understand or make out what he was saying. Finally, we grabbed one of the guys from Happy Hill and asked him if he could help us. He began to ask Alphaeus the same questions that Don and I had been asking him, but to no avail. Alphaeus continued to keep his head bowed, uttering something or slightly nodding his head at times. After several more minutes, the brother from Happy Hill looked at us and just shrugged his shoulders. He couldn't understand what Alphaeus was saying either, even having almost put his ear to Alphaeus' mouth. I just stood there, praying silently that God would help us. We were at a loss. Finally, we summoned Pastor Houston, the Pastor at Happy Hill, to come over. He began talking to Alphaeus and though his head stayed bowed and his words were faint, it seemed that Pastor Houston was actually having a conversation with him. Several more minutes went by and I remember Pastor Houston saying let's pray. I could tell Alphaeus was praying, but I still wasn't completely sure what was happening. They raised their heads and Pastor Houston informed us that Alphaeus had just prayed to receive Jesus as his Savior. Hallelujah! Praise the Lord! That's awesome! Yee-Haw!!! We were absolutely beside ourselves! As we stood there and talked with Alphaeus, who still spoke very quietly, you could see the change on his face. Pastor Houston began to explain to us why Alphaeus was acting the way he was. Alphaeus had told him that the area he lived in was known for a lot of demonic activity and that his brother had just died and he believed it was in some demonic ritual or activity. He went on to tell Pastor Houston that every time we would ask him about trusting Jesus, he felt like there was a fire in his stomach. It frightened him and that is why he would just nod his head and spoke very quietly. But, God is bigger folks! Much bigger! It hit us, that we had just witnessed a serious healing. I believe even though we prayed it wouldn't rain, God knew the heart behind it and blessed us that Old Year's Night with His presence and power. By the way, Alphaeus' girlfriend also accepted Christ that night. Praise the Lord for His blessings!

It was now midnight. We spent some time praying in the new year, thanking God for the year He gave us in 2012, for what we had witnessed this night and for His blessings on our 2013. We packed everything up and around 1:00 a.m., we headed for the hotel. The sleep would be short that night, but oh, was it sweet. For healing to be a part of your ministry and you should want it to be a part of your ministry, it requires living on the aisle. Faith Prays for the Afflicted. Preach with boldness, pray with faith, and don't get caught watching the clouds go by.

Pray Through

"And Jesus came and spake unto them, saying, All power is given unto me in heaven and in earth. Go ye therefore, and teach all nations, baptizing them in the name of the Father, and of the Son, and of the Holy Ghost: Teaching them to observe all things whatsoever I have commanded you: and, lo, I am with you always, even unto the end of the world. Amen." (Matthew 28:18-20)

CHAPTER 4

What a Big Difference a Few Feet Makes

"But when he **saw** the multitudes"
— MATTHEW 9:36 —

A few feet can make a world of difference. Try this the next time you fly. On two separate flights, but close to equal in time and distance, choose the window seat on one flight and the aisle seat on the other flight. Now, if you are like my dad and can't sit still for a minute, he is usually right in the center of the chaos in the aisle, then this probably won't work. But, see if you notice the difference in viewpoint just a few feet makes.

It's Sunday, October 5th, and our first full day in Hyderabad. And, my first time experiencing India in the daytime. Our flight to Mumbai landed late in the evening, I slept all day from the jet-lag, and then our flight to Hyderabad was in the evening as well. Our time in Hyderabad was to be the first of three stops. But, as I will explain later, it becomes the first of only two stops. I'll just say now, listen to God if He wants to change your plans. I was glad we listened. Our contact in Hyderabad was Pastor Wilson. Pastor Wilson was the Pastor of Faith Baptist Church, which he started, and is now the Pastor of Calvary Baptist Church, a sister church he planted out of FBC. He also founded the organization, Advance India. Advance India is involved in planting churches in the city and in the outlying remote villages, running the Grace Harvest Orphans Home, Pastoral support through Bible training, fellowship, and prayer, and the Grace After School Clubs. I'll touch more on that in chapter 10.

Meeting Pastor Wilson was exciting, but definitely a walk by faith moment. I had been corresponding with him for close to three years, but only through Facebook. We had never met or even spoken by phone. I did have one contact here in the U.S. that works with him, so I didn't feel I was going into the trip completely blind. Pastor Wilson met us at our hotel for breakfast and we spent about an hour getting to know each other before we left for our first church service.

When we left the hotel, I couldn't believe the amount of people in the streets and the traffic, though it was a Sunday and the traffic was "supposedly" light. Cars, motorcycles, taxis motorized rickshaws, buses, trucks, and even bicycles, all fighting to make their way through the streets. Everyone honking, weaving back and forth as at times the one lane was four vehicles wide, it seemed. It was chaos in motion. This was the aisle seat. God took the multitudes and brought them into clear view. He took the overall picture I was looking at and brought it into focus. Now, the people were right outside my window, just feet, even inches away. Their faces now I saw in detail. Men, women, boys, girls, young, old. No longer just mass confusion in motion, but now slowed, as if God was saying, do you see the need around you? The faces looked busy, some seemingly searching, and many tired and worn. Now, do I believe Jesus knew everything that was going on around Him? Yes! He is God after all. I believe He is showing an example, painting the picture I had just seen. It was a multitude in need, and when I say need, I'm referring to spiritual need, it was all around us and yet unaware. What caused Jesus to change what He was doing? Let's take a look and see. I think it comes down to the difference a few feet makes.

When it was time for Jesus' ministry to begin, He jumped right into the aisle seat. Performing many miracles and healing a lot of people. One stands out, though, because a few feet made all the difference.

Take time to read the account in **Mark 2:1-12**. Jesus was back in Capernaum, His base, His home during His years of ministry. Capernaum was a "metropolis" (if you will) of Galilee situated near the northwest corner of the Sea of Galilee. Capernaum was a prosperous town and very crowded. You might say, a great place for a great harvest. Capernaum comes from the Greek, Kapernaoum which means, "city of comfort." The perfect place for Jesus to be, wouldn't you agree?

Jesus was at the house (v. 1), probably Peter's house, and word got out that He was back in town. Because of the miracles and healings Jesus was performing, He began to draw crowds, big crowds, wherever He went. I'm sure Jesus was there just relaxing for a bit, maybe getting a bite to eat before He headed back out. After all. He had been gone for several days travelling around Galilee. So, as He was sitting there, word began getting around town that He was at the house.

Immediately, it tells us in verse 2, people started gathering at the house. They piled in to hear what Jesus had to say and, in no time, the house was completely full. It was so full, it says they stood outside the door and listened. I can picture it in my mind. People pressing against each other, trying to get a glimpse of Jesus through the door or a window opening. Come on! Move man, let me get a look! What is Jesus saying? I just want to hear what He is saying.

Then comes an amazing show of faith. Four men show up (v. 3) carrying their friend who had the palsy. He couldn't walk, so there was no way he could get to Jesus without help. Of course they were late getting to where Jesus was, having to carry their friend all the way there on his bed. Think of the conversation they must have had with their friend. Just hold on buddy, we're almost there! Jesus will heal you, we know He will. We just have to get close to Him! But, there was no getting close. The crowd was so big, they couldn't even get close to the house. I can imagine, "Excuse me please. We need to get through. Our friend needs to see Jesus so He can heal him. Please! Please just give us some room!" The crowd, probably a little annoyed at these guys, were probably saying, "Back off guys! We were here first! Be quiet! We're trying to hear Jesus!" Interesting isn't it? They didn't "see" this man with the palsy the way Jesus would have seen him. The crowd was there for the show. It seems the church crowd today, too often, is just there for the show too. Do we even stop to "see" those around us or is it, get in, get what I want, and get out?

These four friends of the man with the palsy were determined, though. They were going to get to Jesus one way or another. And, what verse 4 tells us they did, was unbelievable. You talk about thinking outside the box. Most people would have quit when they couldn't get in the door or maybe through a window. Not these guys! Nope! I can just see it. One of the guys says, "I've got an idea, follow me." They head around to the back of the house because there isn't a door or windows in the back (that's not scripture, just how my mind sees it). Somehow, they work themselves up to the rooftop and have gotten their friend up there too. I'll let you think that one through. They begin to tear the roof off, broke it in pieces until they have made a gigantic hole in the roof. This is where I think it has to be Peter's house. Peter, the guy who ran his mouth all the time. To me, this shows God's sense of humor. Peter would be sitting there, not wanting to interrupt Jesus, but in his head he's screaming, "What are you doing to my roof? You guys are going to pay to fix that! You've got to be kidding me!" Then, these four men, it says, begin to lower their friend down right in front of Jesus. These guys are awesome! Who wouldn't want these four guys as friends. But, I have to ask, where did they get the rope to lower him down? I'm telling you, when you read scripture, picture it. Put yourself there. It makes it mean so much more, I believe. Was the rope just "coincidentally" laying behind the house? Why would they have brought rope if they were going to take their friend in through the door? There is no way when they picked up their friend, that one of them said, "Hey, grab some rope just in case we have to go on the roof and bust a big hole in it and lower Johnny down that way." Is this faith or what? I'm sure people were getting upset when pieces of the roof were falling on their head. The noise of tearing the roof apart would have been distracting. And then a guy being lowered down right on top of where many would have been standing, forcing them to move back. But, these four guys said, we have to get our friend in front of Jesus so he can be healed. What lengths will you and I go to get a friend or family member or someone we come in contact with who is lost, in front of Jesus. Well. If we truly "see" them and believe, as these four guys did, that Jesus is the only hope one has, then I imagine we would go to pretty great lengths to get that person to Jesus.

The house that was all a buzz a few seconds earlier, I bet is so silent now you could hear a pin drop. What's going on, people must have been whispering to one another? And of course, the "religious" bunch in the room must have been beside themselves. Who does this paralyzed guy think he is interrupting our trying to hear Jesus say something so we can hate him more (vv. 6-7)? How dare he! Oh, but don't miss verse 5. As the man with the palsy was being lowered, Jesus stopped preaching, the house became silent, and Jesus just stared up at those four men with, I bet, the biggest smile on His face. That is what verse 5 says! "When Jesus saw their faith." When Jesus looked up, He why these guys were doing what they were doing. He saw in their faces the faith, the belief, that Jesus was the Son of God and could heal their friend. And, oh, did Jesus heal him! But, not quite how you might think. It says when Jesus saw the faith of the four men, he looked at the paralyzed man and said, "Son, thy sins be forgiven thee." Whoa! Hold on a minute! Stop the presses! Jesus just healed this man spiritually! I thought the four guys brought him to be physically healed (we'll see what happens there in a minute). Well, they did bring him for that, but they knew that their friend needed more than just the physical healing. He was lost and needed saved. He was dead and now is alive. What a celebration that took place on that rooftop that day. Have you ever prayed for a friend or loved one to be saved and you brought them to church and they got saved? I believe God does that sometimes because He sees our faith. I believe God wants us to not just pray that a person will get saved, but to make whatever effort we need to, to get them to Jesus so He will save (heal) them. I love how Jesus called him "Son", because he was now God's child, before He even told him he was forgiven of his sins. That is how fast faith makes you a child of God. Before I cried out to God at the age of 19 to save me, He saw my faith and was already calling me His son. And, he did the same for you if you are His child and if you are not yet, He is patiently waiting for you to come to Him so He can utter those same words He said to the paralyzed man, "Son thy sins be forgiven thee."

You may be reading this book and God is beginning to reveal that to you, that you need to be healed spiritually. You are realizing you've never truly come to Christ in faith. Would you please stop for a moment and allow me to lower you down in front of Jesus? Maybe you're not even sure what it means or what to do. I want to help you. Consider these 4 S's from Romans:

<u>Si</u>n – "For all have sinned and come short of the glory of God." (Romans 3:23)

<u>S</u>eparation – "For the wages of sin is death;" (Romans 6:23)

<u>S</u>olution – "But God commendeth his love toward us, in that, while we were yet sinners, Christ died for us." (Romans 5:8)

<u>S</u>alvation – "That if thou shalt confess with thy mouth the Lord Jesus, and shalt believe in thine heart that God hath raised him from the dead, thou shalt be saved. For with the heart man believeth unto righteousness; and with the mouth confession is made unto salvation. For whosoever shall call upon the name of the Lord shall be saved." (Romans 10:9-10, 13)

Praise the Lord, He makes it that simple. If that is where you are at right now, stop and take a minute to pray to God. Confess your sin to Him. Believe that Jesus died for your sins, was buried and rose again the third day and while you cry out to God to save you, know that He is already calling you "son". Welcome to the family brother! sister! Put your bookmark here and come back later. Right now, go celebrate what God has done in your life. Tell your family or your Pastor (if you have one). Call a friend and let them know the good news and, hey, if they don't know Jesus, tell them you want to introduce them. All you need to remember are the 4 S's. It's that easy. I'll be here, with a big smile on my face, waiting for you to get back.

Welcome Back! I hope you had a good time celebrating with Jesus! So, how do things end with this house gathering in Capernaum. Well, as I mentioned earlier, the "religious" twits get all bothered by what has taken place and the fact that Jesus has essentially said He is God by forgiving the paralyzed man's sins. Of course they don't actually say anything which is standard practice, but Jesus, because He is God, knows what they are thinking and rebukes them for it (vv. 6-9). He did this so the man with the palsy would know and understand that Jesus is God, the only one who can forgive sins (v. 10). Jesus then proceeds to physically heal the paralyzed man (vv.11-12). God healed his physical body and his spiritual body all in the same day. As soon as Jesus told the paralyzed man to "get up", verse 12 says he immediately got up and like the Red Sea, the crowd parted as the once paralyzed man walked out of the house carrying his own bed. How stinkin' awesome is that? And, so the day ended just as it always should when we've been in the presence of God and seen Him work. The end of verse 12 says it this way, "insomuch that they were all amazed, and glorified God, saying, We never saw it on this fashion." Translation: Eyes bugged out and jaws dropped and God was glorified, He was praised, His name was lifted up when the people all said to each other, "I ain't seen nothin' like that!"

Pray Through

"Jesus said unto him, Thou shalt love the Lord thy God with all thy heart, and with all thy soul, and with all thy mind. This is the first and great commandment. And the second is like unto it, Thou shalt love thy neighbor as thyself. On these two commandments hang all the law and the prophets." (Matthew 22:37-40)

CHAPTER 5

Hit by the Food Cart

"he was **moved** with compassion on them,"
— MATTHEW 9:36 —

If you ever get hit by the food cart on a plane, it will cause you to do one thing...Move! We had several food cart moments in India. Those moments that become seared in your mind forever.

After a day and a half spent in our hotel in Hyderabad due to illness, I'll share more about that in chapter 7, Peter and I decided to get out, go for a little walk and catch some fresh air. Though, with all the fumes and the stench from all the trash that is thrown anywhere and everywhere, the air was anything but fresh. But, we had been cooped up in the hotel, so at least the walk would do us good. As we walked along, we decided we would cross the street and check out a couple shops (souvenirs for the family help when you're gone from home this long). This was the first food cart moment for me. You see, crossing the street isn't a passive undertaking in India. Remember, the food cart makes you move. We stepped out into the street and immediately I was thrust into the game, Frogger. Now, I know I'm dating myself a little and for those of you who have no idea what Frogger is, go google it. Move forward, slide to the right, one step back, slide back to the left, two steps forward, on and on until you reach the other side, hopefully without getting smashed to the pavement.

Sunday morning in Hyderabad. As we left the hotel, heading to the first of three church services where Peter and I would be speaking, Pastor Wilson told us he wanted to pass through one of the slum areas where they minister. As we made our way through town, we turned down a side street. Pastor Wilson pointed out the slum area off to our left. Between it and us was a waterway, like a small river or brook. Pastor Wilson explained to us that the waterway was actually the sewage draining from the city and that the government gave the people this land to build their shacks (if that is even a good term for them) because no one else would ever build anything next to it. Try to imagine living everyday with the smell, which, with each slight breeze or gust of wind, was absolutely overwhelming. Imagine the murky water, littered with trash and filled with human waste flowing right outside your home. You can't can you? That's when I saw him. A little boy, probably three or four years old. He didn't have any clothes on and he was squatting at the top of the bank of this filthy sewage way. He was pooping! Right there on the ground! Right out in the open! This wasn't a little boy who just decided he wanted to go to the bathroom outside. This was his life. He has basically been told he's no different than the animals that roamed around him. When you have to go, just go! This was the mentality, concerning all aspects of life that dominated the slums. This was a definite food cart moment. I'll share more about this work being done in the slum areas later in the book.

It was Tuesday evening. Peter was feeling better, so we decided to visit one of the Grace After School Clubs which Pastor Wilson had started in another slum area of Hyderabad. It was being held in a church started by one of the local Pastor's, who lived in this particular slum. As we pulled up to the entrance of the slum, which was home to hundreds of thousands of people, Pastor Wilson did a little confessing. He told Peter and me, though he has visited the club many times, he still wasn't exactly sure how to get to it. My first thought was, finally, I'm not the only one completely lost here! But, immediately, my thought went to, but I am completely lost here and you are the one who is supposed to be showing me the way. Fortunately, the cavalry showed up, in the form of a ten year old little girl. The Pastor of the church pulled up on his motorcycle (a very common form of transportation in India), dropped his daughter off, and she showed us the way through the slum to where the club was meeting. I quickly learned why we parked outside the slum. The paths, they were definitely not streets, were too narrow for even a small car like Pastor Wilson's to navigate. You could only navigate through the slum on motorbikes, bicycles, or by walking. It was like a maze, a huge maze! Man, I felt like one of those mice trying to find my way to the piece of cheese. I would have loved to have had an aerial photo of that area just to see what the maze looks like. Peter and I got to share about Jesus to the 20-30 kids who were there, which included many Hindu and Muslim children. They sang songs about Jesus and quoted scripture verses. What precious kids. What a great night! What a food cart moment!

One of the most powerful verses in the Bible, in my opinion, just happens to also be the shortest verse in the Bible. John 11:35 simply, but powerfully says, "Jesus wept." The power and enormity of this verse is seen in that Jesus was "moved". To weep means to cry intensely. It's not just something that brings a tear to your eye. No, this is down on your knees, hands on your face, almost uncontrollably crying. What on earth could bring Jesus to the point of weeping? Before I explain what it was that caused Jesus to weep, take a few minutes and read John 11.

We know that Lazarus and his two sisters, Mary and Martha were very special people to Jesus. Verse 2 of John 11 tells us, "(It was that Mary which anointed the Lord with ointment, and wiped his feet with her hair,". Verse 3 says "...Lord, behold, he (translated, your dear friend) whom thou lovest is sick." And verse 5 says, "Now Jesus loved Martha, and her sister, and Lazarus." I think it is safe to say that, yes, Jesus really loved this family.

So, Lazarus has fallen sick, and, it must be pretty serious, because Mary and Martha sent word for Jesus to come (v. 3). Now, knowing how much Jesus loved Lazarus, we would assume he got the fellas together and hit the road right away. But, that's not what happened. Actually, it was just the opposite. Verse 4 tells us that when Jesus heard that Lazarus was sick, really sick, His response was, "This sickness is not unto death,". What? Mary and Martha said Lazarus was really sick and it doesn't look like he's going to make it. Hurry Jesus! Get here right away! It goes on to say, in verse 6, "When he (Jesus) had heard therefore that he (Lazarus) was sick, he abode two days still in the same place where he was." If you are like me, you begin to think, does anything move Jesus? Does Jesus really love these guys? Weird way to show it, isn't it?

This must be that whole, "His ways are not our ways and His thoughts are higher than our thoughts" thing! That is actually scriptural (See Isaiah 55:9). We don't think like Jesus! We don't do things the way He does! He is God, we are not. So, why did Jesus seemingly blow off this urgent 9-1-1 call from Mary and Martha. Look back at verse 4 in John 11. After Jesus told His disciples that Lazarus wasn't going to die from this sickness, He shares why He is going to do what He's about to do. It says, "but for the glory of God, that the Son of God might be glorified (honored) thereby." At the end of the day, when all is said and done, what will take place, Jesus says, will glorify me. That's how it should be.

After the two days of waiting, Jesus goes to the disciples and says, alright, let's go see Lazarus. He tells them, "Our friend Lazarus sleepeth; but I go, that I may awake him out of sleep (v. 11). Now these guys are really confused. They're texting each other smh (shake my head), I think Jesus is losing it! If Lazarus is sick, isn't it good if he is resting? Why would you want to wake him up, Jesus? Let him get some rest so he will start feeling better (see v. 12). Of course, Jesus was probably shaking His head and thinking, man these guys don't get it. So, He tells them "plainly" in verse 14, so they will get it, "Lazarus is dead." Jesus tells them it's ok though. He tells them it's actually a good thing they didn't go right away because they, also, need to believe who Jesus says He is and He's going to show them something that might help them believe. You always have that one guy, though, that has to put his two cents in. Usually with this bunch, it was Peter, right? Always running his mouth at the wrong time and in the wrong place. Not this time, however. This time it is Thomas. Remember, Jesus had a target on His back and these guys were nervous about travelling away from their current location because they felt safe where they were. So,

Thomas spouts off to the rest of the guys in verse 16 (and I paraphrase), Great! Let's go with Jesus to see Lazarus' tomb and while we are at it, we'll get killed too! SMH. I can see Jesus being saddened by Thomas' remarks and the disciples' lack of understanding.

As Jesus and the disciples drew close to Bethany, where Lazarus lived, people were telling Him that Lazarus had now "lain in the grave four days already." (v. 17). Word got to Martha that Jesus was coming (v. 20) and she immediately went to where Jesus was. When Martha found Jesus, her first words were, If only you had been here Jesus, my brother would still be alive (v. 21). Is she blaming Jesus for her brother's death? She believed Jesus could have healed him, but I guess only if He was physically there. We see that in what she says to Jesus next, "But I know, that even now, whatsoever thou wilt ask of God, God will give it thee." (v. 22). I wonder if Jesus thought that Martha felt He wasn't quite good enough to handle the situation? I wonder if Jesus ever thinks the same thing about us, about His church. Has the American church in its drive to be "culturally relevant" actually told Jesus, "You're good Jesus, just not quite good enough". I'm just asking! I hear a whole lot these days that the Bible isn't really God's Word. It doesn't really work in our culture today. It's not relevant. The church has moved away from biblical ideas in certain areas. What may have been seen as wrong in Jesus' day, in our day, are acceptable. Aren't we really saying, kind of like Martha did, I love ya Jesus, but you're too late. Your methods would have worked earlier, but they're no good to us now.

Jesus tries to reassure Martha and tells her that Lazarus will rise again (v. 23). Martha (I'm sure not real excited about a Bible lesson at this time) tells Jesus that she knows he will rise again in the resurrection (v. 24). Like the disciples earlier, Martha believes, but she's just not fully getting it. She doesn't understand what Jesus is telling her when He says, "I am the resurrection, and the life, he that believeth in me, though he were dead, yet shall he live." (v.25). He is telling Martha that He's about to blow her mind. Martha confesses that Jesus is the Christ, the Son of God (v. 27), but walks off as if to say, but that doesn't do me any good right now. My brother is dead! This adds to Jesus' sorrow.

Mary came racing, verse 29, to see Jesus after Martha had informed her that Jesus was just outside the city. She was so eager to see Jesus, that it caused many of the people who had been grieving with her to come too (v. 31). Mary, the one who had anointed Jesus and washed His feet with her hair. The one who truly saw and understood who Jesus was. Jesus must have thought (He already knew how she would respond), finally someone who will understand my plan. Nope! Mary ran up to Jesus and fell down at His feet (v. 32), a glimpse of the faith she had when she anointed Him. But, like all of the rest, her grief caused her faith to waver and she said to Jesus, "...if thou hadst been here, my brother had not died." (v. 32). Just like Martha, her testimony to all those around was, you're good Jesus, just not quite good enough. How Jesus must have grieved to hear Mary utter those words. How Jesus must feel as His church, by their actions, utter the same words. Martha, Mary, the disciples, they knew Jesus. They believed Jesus was the Christ. They weren't just acquaintances. These were His close friends, the ones that knew Him best. You, me, the church, we know Jesus. We have His word. It tells us all about Him. We're not just acquaintances. We are His children, so we say. We should know Him better than anyone. So, how does Jesus feel? Verse 33 tells us as Jesus watched Mary weeping and the others that had come with her, weeping, "...he groaned in the spirit, and was troubled." (v. 33). Translated, *He was deeply **moved***. And, then we see it, the enormity of the situation. The great love Jesus had for the people, though they didn't understand, they didn't fully trust. They didn't really see Him. As they walked off to show Jesus where Lazarus was laid, scripture tells us, "Jesus wept." (v.35). A moment that caused the people to stop and acknowledge, "...Behold how he loved him!" (v. 36). I pray you and I will stop for a moment to acknowledge how much Jesus loves us. "But God commendeth (**showed**) his love toward us, in that, while we were yet sinners, Christ died for us." (Romans 5:8). "For God so loved the world, that he gave his only begotten Son, that whosoever believeth in him should not perish, but have everlasting life." (John 3:16).

In true Christ-like fashion, Jesus did what He came to do, glorify God. With people still questioning Him (v. 37) and thinking He was nuts for wanting to open Lazarus' tomb (vv. 38-39), Jesus said to them, "...Said I not unto thee, if thou wouldest believe, thou shouldest see the *glory of God.*" (v. 40) (*emphasis added*). I promise, if you will just believe me, I will blow your socks off! They moved the stone from the opening of the tomb and Jesus prayed (vv. 41-42). Father, I know you hear me. You **always** hear me! But, I'm praying here out loud so that these folks will believe that you sent me here and that I am your Son. What was He saying? That the people would believe He was God. You want to unleash the glory of God in your life? Just pray and believe that He (Jesus) is God (Stop and read John 1:1)! So, with that, it says that Jesus "cried with a loud voice" (v. 43), LAZARUS, COME ON OUT OF THERE MY FRIEND! Picture in your mind the looks on the peoples' faces when, "he that was dead came forth" (v. 44). YEE-HAW!!! Jesus had to call Lazarus by name or else everyone who had ever died would have come walking out of their graves. That is the power of God! That is what happens when Jesus is "moved"! Think about the impact God could make in this world through our lives, if we were "moved".

Scripture tells us that many that day "believed on him" (v. 45), but that some "went their ways to the Pharisees" (v. 46). A bunch of "religious" tattletales! I pray today that in your life and in mine, we will let God "move" us with compassion for others. I pray we will be faithful to take the truth of the Gospel (death, burial and resurrection of Jesus) to a lost world, so we may see "dead" people come forth to "life" eternal in Christ. The results? Well, those are up to God.

Pray Through

"These things I have spoken unto you, that in me ye might have peace, in the world ye shall have tribulation: but, be of good cheer; I have overcome the world." (John 16:33)

CHAPTER 6

The View from the Aisle Seat

"because they fainted, and were scattered
abroad, as sheep having no shepherd."
— MATTHEW 9:36 —

India is a very religious country. Now, on the surface, you might say
that's good. But, remember, there is a big difference between religion
and a relationship (specifically with Jesus Christ). Hinduism makes up
80% of India's population. Some of their key beliefs are:

- **Truth is eternal** – Hindus pursue knowledge and understanding
  of the Truth: the very essence of the universe and the only
  Reality. According to the Vedas (their scripture), Truth is One,
  but the wise express it in a variety of ways.
- **Brahman is Truth and Reality** – Hindus believe in Brahman
  as the one true God who is formless, limitless, all-inclusive,
  and eternal. Brahman is not an abstract concept; it is a real
  entity that encompasses everything (seen and unseen) in the
  universe.
- **The Vedas are the ultimate authority** – Vedas are Hindu
  scriptures which contain revelations received by ancient saints
  and sages. The Vedas are without beginning or end. When
  everything else in the universe is destroyed (at the end of a
  cycle of time), the Vedas remains.

- **Everyone should strive to achieve dharma** – Dharma can be described as right conduct, righteousness, moral law, and duty. Anyone who makes dharma central to one's life strives to do the right thing, according to one's duties and abilities, at all times.
- **Individual souls are immortal** – A Hindu believes that the individual soul (*atman*) is neither created nor destroyed; it has been, it is, and it will be. Actions of the soul while residing in a body require that it reap the consequences of those actions in the next life – the same soul in a different body. The process of movement of the atman from one body to another is known as *transmigration*. The kind of body the soul inhabits next is determined by *karma* (actions accumulated in previous lives).
- **The goal of the individual soul is moksha** – Moksha is liberation: the soul's release from the cycle of death and rebirth. It occurs when the soul unites with Brahman by realizing its true nature. Several paths can lead to this realization and unity: the path of duty, the path of knowledge, and the path of devotion (unconditional surrender to Brahman).

Muslims make up 14% of the population. Muslims have six main beliefs and five Pillars. The six main beliefs are:

- Belief in Allah as the one and only God
- Belief in angels
- Belief in the holy books (Qur'an)
- Belief in the Prophets: Adam, Ibrahim (Abraham), Musa (Moses), Dawud (David), Isa (Jesus), Muhammad (peace be upon him) is the final prophet
- Belief in the Day of Judgment – The day when the life of every human being will be assessed to decide whether they go to heaven or hell.
- Belief in Predestination – That Allah has the knowledge of all that will happen. Muslims believe that this doesn't stop human beings from making free choices.

The five Pillars which are essential to their faith include:

- **Shahada** –to declare one's faith in God and belief in Muhammad
- **Salat** – to pray five times a day (at dawn, noon, afternoon, sunset, and evening)
- **Zakat** – to give to those in need
- **Sawm** – to fast during Ramadan (a holy month of fasting, introspection and prayer that celebrates the month during which they believe Muhammad received the initial revelations of the Qur'an)
- **Hajj** – to make a pilgrimage to Mecca at least once during a person's lifetime if the person is able.

Of the remaining 6% of the population, only 0.8% belong to an Evangelical or gospel believing work. Hundreds of millions of people trusting in a god(s) that cannot give any hope. Let that sink in for a minute! All of these people think they are ok or will be ok at some point! I'm good because I believe in this god or that god, or when I die, there will be those who will help pray me in, only to realize it is too late when they hear those fate sealing words from the Lord Jesus Christ, "Depart from me, I never knew you." (Matthew 7:23, 25:41, Luke 13:27). See, my relationship with God is just that, my relationship. Only I can call upon the name of the Lord for salvation (see Romans 10:13). It is my responsibility (see Romans 14:12). No one can do it for me. When I leave this earth (when I die), my eternity is set, no go backs. I won't stand before God and He will make a determination on heaven or hell for me, whether I've been good enough for His heaven. I could never be good enough (see Romans 3:10-11). That is decided in this life we have on earth. Based on our decision in this life, scripture tells us we will either stand before the Judgment Seat of Christ (2 Corinthians 5:10) or The Great White Throne Judgment (Revelation 20:11-15). Take a minute and also read Matthew 25:31-46 on this subject. Back to the information I shared about religion in India. This is just one country! Multiply that throughout the entire world. Are you starting to "see"? Are you beginning to be "moved"? It only means something if you really see it, are moved by it, and then act on it. This, my friend, is the view from the aisle seat.

Let me give you an example of what I mean by SEE, MOVED, ACT. My friend Peter and I prayed that God would really reveal Himself and help us see the need we would experience while we were traveling to the different parts of India. During our time in Bhadrachalam with Remote Tribal Missions (RTM), we visited an orphanage, then a tribal village in the jungle, but it was our last stop that really drove this home to me.

SEE - As we drove into the village to meet some folks from the church that worked with RTM, God, as He had done at the other places we visited, was allowing me to see the things around me. I mean, like, notice the details. One way He was doing that was through Pastor Wilson. As he would explain different things, the picture was being painted in my mind. We passed a row of huts, home to the villagers. They were simple one room dwellings. No great architectural design, fancy roof lines or beautiful paint jobs. I, like most Americans I assume would, had a hard time even imagining what it would be like to live in something like that. I don't mean to sound degrading, but it's just the truth. We wouldn't know what to do if we had to pile our family into one pretty small area where you cooked, watched tv, slept, did everything. Speaking of watching tv, another thing that caught my eye, was that every hut had a satellite dish mounted on it. Yep, that's right, they had satellite tv. According to Pastor Wilson, the Government provided these to the people, probably in exchange for something else that was of more benefit to the Government than the satellite dishes were to the people. As we rounded the bend, we could see the church up ahead. Again, a very simply constructed building. In front of the church and pouring into the street must have been the whole village, or at least it seemed so. They had all come out to greet Peter and me. It was as if the President or the Queen was visiting. They were playing instruments and waving things in the air. Thankfully, the video that Peter shot of me dancing with all the people can't be put in a book! I really felt kind of bad because, well, it was just Peter and me. I felt like they should be really disappointed, but they weren't. They were so excited we were there, that we had come to see them. But, honestly, I was just as excited to be there and see them. I loved that God allowed me to see the beauty of the people and especially the kids. I loved the conversation that God and I had as He spoke to my spirit, saying, this is my creation too, Tony. Aren't they magnificent? Aren't they absolutely stunning? Look at their amazing smiles. Look deep into their beautiful eyes. Don't miss them, Tony. I love them dearly. See them as I see them. My response in my mind was, I see them, God! I see them, I do! Wow! You are so amazing, God! You are so amazing! I couldn't help but think, amongst the simplicity of construction stood the magnificence of creation.

Moved – My spirit was churning. The flood of emotions from what I was seeing overwhelmed me. I was so excited to meet these folks and to have the opportunity to speak with them for a few minutes inside the church building. I was humbled that they treated us like we were the most important people in the world, adorning us with these beautiful linen wraps, and that whatever we had to say to them was of the utmost importance. The first couldn't be further from the truth, but the second was right on, whether they realized it yet or not. I'll share more about speaking to them in the section on ACT. As we pulled up in front of the church and began to step out of the vehicle we were travelling in, my excitement, and all that I had imagined in my mind, became a reality. People flocked around, shaking our hands and greeting us with hugs. The kids began holding our hands and embracing us. That, the reaction from the kids, is what began to pull at my heart strings. I thought about how Jesus was always ready to meet with the kids. How He loved them so much and cautioned people, even His disciples at one point, to be careful how they treated the kids. I was truly excited to meet all of these folks, but honestly, I was most excited to get to hang out with the kids of the village. I love kids! I am so thankful that God has allowed me to minister and serve in the area of youth ministry. I began to understand, it is when you really "see", by focusing on the people, feeling their touch as they grab your hand or feeling the texture of their hair as you place your hand on the head of a child embracing you, that you are truly "moved". Their need becomes your heart.

ACT – When you see a person as God sees them and are moved by their condition, situation, or need, then you are compelled to act. I don't mean you think you ought to do something, no, I mean, you do something! Doing something can manifest itself in many ways. You can grab a ladle and dish out some food to hungry kids. You embrace a child, as Jesus did, and tell them you love them, even though you've never met them before (I pray even today, that those kids I met in that village think about that man from a far-away country that loves them). You take hold of a child's hand reaching for yours even though, as a friend at church put it, "You know where that hand has been." But, you hold it anyway. You dance with them, even when a man about your age grabs your hand for way too long to teach you their dance (and it all gets caught on tape by your "friend"). You just dance. And then, after you've tried to show them the best you can that you love them, you tell them about the One who loves them beyond what is humanly possible, a love beyond their wildest imagination. Jesus! After the festivities took place outside, and believe me, it was festive, we made our way into the church. It was there that I got to take a few minutes and share the simple, but oh so important message of the Gospel with them. I looked back and forth into the eyes of those kids and told them that they and I were the same. In God's eyes, we are no different. We both had the same problem and the problem is sin (I shared Romans 3:23 with them). I shared with them that our sin separates us from God (I quoted Romans 6:23 to them). Then I told them that Jesus loved them and me and the whole world so much that He died on a cross to pay for our sins (Romans 5:8). I told them that was great news because if they would confess their sin to Jesus and they would believe with all their heart that Jesus died for their sins, was buried, and rose again the third day, then Jesus would save them and one day they would live in Heaven with Jesus (I read Romans 10:9-10 to them and quoted John 3:16). I told them all they had to do was ask Jesus (and I quoted Romans 10:13). You know how you can be sure that your ACT is genuine, sincere, God blessed? When years later, if you close your eyes, you can still "see" all the details and as you think on it, your heart is "moved" all over again.

Our text for this chapter is Matthew 9:36, "because they fainted, and were scattered abroad, as sheep having no shepherd." This is what caused Jesus to show compassion. To finish this chapter, I want to focus not on the "fainted" and "scattered", but instead, on the compassionate Shepherd that tends to and loves them.

In my Bible, the section of John 10:1-21 is entitled, "I Am the Good Shepherd". Take a moment to read this scripture and then let's look at how good our shepherd truly is.

(1-2) I am thankful for this door that our shepherd has put in place to keep us, His sheep, protected in all ways. We see right away that there are those, called "a thief and a robber", that will try to get to the sheep by climbing over or around the door. As we will see later, this thief is none other than the devil himself. These first two verses are great reminders for us. God, the Shepherd, always comes through the main door of our heart. The devil, thief and robber, can't come through that door, so he has to try to sneak in another way. His entry is often through our eyes, our thoughts, our feelings, our pride.

(3-4) The gate-keeper knows exactly who to let in. Can't you just picture a bunch of excited sheep when they hear their shepherd's voice? They know he has come to lead them out of their pen in to green pasture. The shepherd is so protective of his sheep that he won't just let them run off. In verse three it says he "leadeth them out". In verse four it says "he goeth before them". The sheep love and trust the shepherd so much that they "follow him". And, why wouldn't they? He is going to take them where they can eat and drink water in abundance. They will be nourished and grow. That is exactly what God wants for you and me. He wants us to be nourished and grow in our faith and He promises us He will lead us to the best pastures if we will trust and follow Him. Can you hear His voice calling you? Do you recognize it?

(5) How does the devil sometimes get in around or over the door? Too often, the sheep listen to the wrong voice. As sheep, who are vulnerable, it is vital that we recognize the voice of our Shepherd. It truly is a matter of life or death. When we hear the voice of someone other than the Shepherd, we should recognize the difference and flee from him. Why? Because we know it is the voice of a thief or robber. Don't these first five

verses make a whole lot of sense? Hopefully these words mean life for us, but they didn't to the "religious" leaders of Jesus' day.

(**6**) THEY DID NOT GET IT!

(**7-9**) Jesus had to explain to them that He is the door for the sheep. What is Jesus saying? He is saying that He is the only way to salvation. I pray that we will do as the sheep do when others try to come and lead us away. In verse 8, it says, "but the sheep did not hear them". They didn't listen to the other voices. When the devil tries to lead us in the wrong direction, which is the only way he can lead us, we have to stop listening to him. That path is dangerous and never leads to anything good. It keeps you lost and famished. Jesus says if we will come through Him, we will "be saved" and "find pasture", be nourished.

(**10**) So, here are your options. You can go with satan, the "thief", but his plan is to steal you from Jesus for the great (NOT) purpose of killing and destroying you, which he does subtly. Or, you can go with Jesus whose plan is to give you life and life to the fullest measure. Exactly why do we want to follow the thief so often? The next time he comes calling, ask him this question.

(**11**) Will you die for me? The text you will get back will simply say, LOL! No he won't die for you! His plan is that you will die for him! That's not a good plan, folks! Jesus explains why He is the Good Shepherd. He is good because He gives His life for His sheep. He is more than just willing, He will actually do it. It is what Jesus is telling the people is going to happen, He is going to die for the sins of all people. Why would Jesus do this?

(**12-13**) There is nothing the Shepherd cares for more than His sheep. We see it in how He cares for them versus what scripture calls the "hireling". The sheep don't belong to the hireling, so when trouble comes in the form of a wolf, aka, the devil, that boy runs! He ain't getting killed over a few sheep! He's outta there! Not so with the Shepherd. He stays and fights the wolf. He knows if he doesn't, the wolf will catch them, kill and destroy as we mentioned earlier, and cause them to scatter making them more vulnerable to attack. A sheep that gets separated from the rest of the flock is much easier to catch.

(**14**) Jesus knows every detail of His sheep and His sheep know Him.

The word "shepherd" in this verse refers back to Isaiah 40:11. What comfort this verse gives of the protection and care of the Shepherd. "He shall feed his flock like a shepherd: he shall gather the lambs with his arm, and carry them in his bosom, and shall gently lead those that are with young."

(15) We see the absolute love between the Father and the Son, and Jesus again speaks of the death He will die on the cross for the sins of the world (see Matthew 27:50).

(16) I love this verse and what a challenge it should be to us who are the sheep of the Shepherd. Jesus says there are "other sheep" that aren't in the fold yet. There are more people to be won to Christ, more people that need to hear the great Gospel message, that the Shepherd gave His life for them too. That is the calling you and I have been given, to go tell the message everywhere. Isn't it exciting to know that when we share the Gospel, that person may hear the voice of Jesus and come into His fold? What an unbelievable privilege we have to be God's spokesperson to this world and we can boldly go forth with the great news that JESUS SAVES!

(17-18) Jesus finishes up with the part of His message that always seemed to rub some (usually the "religious" crowd) the wrong way. His message, I am God.

(19-21) Remember what the wolf likes to do? Divide and conquer. The Jewish people again were divided after Jesus spoke. Some thought he was a crazy man, while others began to believe. The message is still the same today, JESUS SAVES! And, the world is still divided over that message. Some believe it is crazy, even full of hate. Others, however, hear the voice of Jesus, that good shepherd, and thankfully enter through the door of life.

Pray Through

"To him the porter openeth; and the sheep hear his voice: and he calleth his own sheep by name, and leadeth them out. (4) And when he putteth forth his own sheep, he goeth before them, and the sheep follow him: for they know his voice." (John 10:3-4)

CHAPTER 7

Flight Diverted

"Then saith he unto his disciples,"
— MATTHEW 9:37 —

Ladies and gentlemen, due to inclement weather, our flight has been diverted and we are going to be landing at... or, due to increased traffic on the ground, the tower has asked us to make a couple of passes before we will be able to land or due to mechanical issues (not the top option of the three) we are going to have to land at the nearest airport and change planes. In simpler terms, what each of these statements is saying is, "Change of plans!". Fortunately, none of these scenarios happened on our flight to India. Our flights were actually all on schedule, which is a huge blessing when traveling that far. We did, however, experience the spiritual version of this. And, if you ask my friend Peter, he would tell you it was the mechanical failure option. Our itinerary was set. Famous last words, I know!

Thursday, October 2, 2014 – Bus ride from Indianapolis, Indiana to Chicago, Illinois – Flight from Chicago to Mumbai (Bombay), India (with stops in Cincinnati, Ohio and Paris, France)

Saturday, October 4, 2014 – Arrive early morning in Mumbai – Spent the day at the home of Peter's relatives – Evening flight to Hyderabad

Sunday & Monday, October 5-6, 2014 – See different ministry needs and opportunities throughout Hyderabad with Pastor Wilson Saripalli, a native Indian pastor

Tuesday, October 7, 2014 – Drive the 8 hour trip to our second ministry stop in Bhadrachalam – Visit local orphanage with Remote Tribal Missions (RTM) Team

Wednesday & Thursday, October 8-9, 2014 – See different ministry needs and opportunities throughout remote tribal areas with RTM Team

Friday, October 10, 2014 – Drive 3-5 hours to Gudivada, our third ministry stop

Saturday & Sunday, October 11-12, 2014 – Visit local orphanages – Speak at a youth event – Speak at a Pastor's conference

Sunday, October 12, 2014 – Drive 6-8 hours back to Hyderabad

Monday, October 13, 2014 – Fly from Hyderabad to Mumbai and then Mumbai to Goa (where Peter grew up and his parents still live)

Tuesday – Thursday, October 14-16, 2014 – Visit with Peter's family and a little relaxation from our busy schedule before heading home

Thursday, October 16, 2014 – Evening flight from Goa to Mumbai

Friday, October 17, 2014 – Fly back home

It was a busy schedule. We had a lot to see in a really short period of time. This was our plan, until…

It was Sunday, October 5 and we were heading out for our first full day in Hyderabad. Pastor Wilson showed up to our hotel early so we could spend a little time talking before we left. This was the first time I had actually met him. It was also the first time we had spoken to each other. Yep, I flew half way around the world to meet a person I had only corresponded with via Facebook. We had messaged for over two years and there was a lot of prayer that went into this trip. We each believed it was God's leading and so we went by faith.

I was still feeling quite jet-lagged, but excited about what was ahead for us in our mission. Peter was still pretty excited, being back in India and having the opportunity to spend some time with his Aunt and cousins in Mumbai. He was also excited to be there just to help me. It really shows his heart. He kept telling me, "I'm here to take care of you, buddy!" Again, famous last words! We stopped briefly in a slum area where Pastor Wilson was trying to restart a work that faltered due to lack of funds. Unfortunately, this is a common theme too often in missions work. But, God is faithful! Then it was off to our first church service. It was unusual for me because in each of the three church services we attended, they had already begun when we arrived and at the first two, after we preached, we left and they continued on. I had the privilege to preach at the first and third church and Peter preached at the second church. Each church was so kind, honoring us with very nice cloth wraps (see pictures) and taking lots of pictures. They like pictures! Peter kept joking with me, saying it had something to do with the white guy in the room! I don't know.

On the way to the third church we stopped at McDonalds, yep, good ol' Mickey D's, to grab a sandwich to go. Peter bought us all Big Macs! You know, two all beef patties, special sauce, lettuce, cheese, pickles, onions, on a sesame seed bun (showing my age again). But, these were Indian Big Macs! So, it was two all chicken patties, spicy mayo, lettuce, tomato, NOT on a sesame seed bun. Hyderabad has a large Hindu population, so in most areas, beef is off limits to eat.

Later that afternoon, Peter and I had a chance to meet with twelve local Pastors. I had the privilege of sharing with them YES Ministries and our vision for seeing youth winning other youth to Christ and then discipling them, that they may go do the same. I asked them to pray for us and that if the Lord wanted us working in India that He would show us in what capacity. We then got a chance to hear from them. I wanted to know their burdens and desires for their individual ministries. I felt like we challenged them, positively, in some areas, especially in the areas of youth evangelism and discipleship. I pray we encouraged them in their faith as much as we were encouraged.

After the Pastor's meeting, we headed to Pastor Wilson's home for dinner. He has a beautiful family. Kind and generous would be two words I would definitely use to describe Pastor Wilson and his family. We ate and ate and ate some more! It was such a sweet time of fellowship and then it was back to the hotel. Back at our room, Peter and I talked about the great first day we experienced on our India mission. It was a long and tiring day, but the excitement of the day ran through our minds over and over. We laughed and joked a little and then hit the lights, excited for what tomorrow would bring, as we were to visit some villages outside of Hyderabad with Pastor Wilson. This is when God said, *"Change of plans!."*

We hadn't been asleep long when I was awakened by that undeniable sound of someone puking their guts up! It was Peter. He wasn't doing well. I think the jet-lag, lack of sleep, and abundance of food (his Aunt and Pastor Wilson's wife fed us like we hadn't eaten in weeks) had finally caught up to him. As the symptoms continued, our level of concern began to grow. The pain he was describing in his stomach reminded him of the time he had food poisoning. He even contemplated going to the hospital. For the next several hours we just sat and prayed and talked, discussing possible changes to our schedule, then Peter would run off to the bathroom again. There was going to be no sleep tonight.

By morning, though absolutely exhausted now, we felt a peace with the change of direction God was showing us. During the night, we decided we would bypass seeing the village ministries the next day and stay at the hotel and rest. Being sick is one thing, but being sick in another country can really be dangerous, even for someone like Peter, who grew up in India, but has lived in the USA for over thirty years now. It's best to be smart and not take the risk. There was no way now we could get to each of the three ministries we had planned to visit. When we put the schedule together, it was tight, to say the least. Since I had put them in the order of my interest, the decision was that we would have to cancel the meeting with the third ministry. Not an easy decision (and not received very well by that ministry), but God showed us it was the right decision. Though we think the plan has changed, God's plan never changed. We learn it was our plans that changed. Sometimes we don't understand this at first. Sometimes we fight it and God has to get our attention to get us back on the right track, His track. The way He gets our attention is often times unpleasant, but it's so cool when you see the "exceeding abundantly" (See Ephesians 3:20) results of His plan. BTW (by the way), they are always so much better!

"And straightway Jesus constrained his disciples to get into a ship, and *to go before him unto the other side*, while he sent the multitudes away." (Matthew 14:22) (Emphasis mine).

Do not miss the middle part of this verse. It is vital. It is key to understanding God's plan. What did Jesus say the plan was? Simple, the plan was for the disciples to take a boat and go to the other side and Jesus would meet them there. Got it? Simple plan, right? The disciples thought so, until…

Jesus had just turned 5 loaves and 2 fishes into a meal for 20,000 plus people. You say, I thought Jesus fed 5,000? Well, scripture tells us it was "5,000 men, beside (*not counting*) women and children." (Matthew 14:21). So, if each man there had a wife and at least two kids, that would be 20,000 plus people who the disciples fed with the meal Jesus prepared from "five loaves, and two fishes" (Matthew 14:17).

After the meal was over, Jesus gives each of His disciples a basket of leftovers (v.20) and tells them to get in the boat and go to the other side and He will meet them there for their next ministry stop. Jesus then begins to send all of the people away and when He is finished doing so, He heads up into the mountain alone to spend some time praying (v. 23).

I can imagine the conversation the disciples were having as they launched out, with their "doggy-bags" of food, heading toward Capernaum. "I can't believe how many people were there and the food never stopped!" "How did Jesus do that?" "That was unbelievable!" "Jesus is amazing! I'll never doubt Him again." That last line must have come from Peter don't you think? But, as the disciples rowed out, things suddenly turned horribly bad, so it seemed. About mid-way across the sea, a huge storm rolled in. Storms come up quickly on the Sea of Galilee and so it was nothing new to most of these guys who spent their lives in their BC (Before Christ) days on these waters as fishermen. But this storm was different. It was like nothing they had experienced before. This storm absolutely scared them to death. Verse 24 tells us, they were being "tossed with waves, for the wind was contrary". Mark 6:48 tells us that Jesus, from His vantage point up in the mountain, "saw them toiling in rowing, for the wind was contrary unto them". Remember though, Jesus never thought, "Man,

I didn't see that storm coming." It was part of His plan. All night, these guys rowed and rowed and went nowhere. The disciples believed this was the end for them. I would say, they have forgotten the plan that Jesus told them about when He said, "I'll meet you on the other side". Maybe they thought the plan had changed and it was for their demise. I wonder if Peter, and the rest, was still not doubting Jesus?

In the "fourth watch" (v. 25), early in the morning, it says Jesus came "walking on the sea". When the disciples saw Him, they didn't realize it was Jesus. The rain and wind would have made visibility almost zero. They thought it was a spirit, a ghost, and it says they "cried out for fear" (v. 26). Oh, but aren't you thankful for the ever-comforting words of Jesus during our times of fear and distress? The storm doesn't cease. Its intensity doesn't let up. When you, like the disciples, are ready to give up, you hear those words, "Be of good cheer, it is I, be not afraid." It's Jesus! He's here! How will you respond?

Of course, Peter jumps to the front and says, Jesus, if that is really you (that's called doubt), let me walk out there to you. Jesus told him to c'mon out and see for himself. I don't know if it was faith or Peter just wanted to look cool in front of the other guys, but whichever it was, you have to give him this, the dude hopped out of the boat. This is the point where, hopefully you are beginning to see what keeps our faith strong and what makes it weak. Verse 29 says that, "he walked on the water, to go to Jesus". What changed for Peter? The storm hadn't stopped. It actually was still going quite strong. What changed was his focus. His focus was now on Jesus and not his circumstance. I believe focusing on Him is what Jesus, in the main text for this book, is wanting us to do. When we focus our efforts on others, begin to "see" them and be "moved" by their circumstances, we are actually seeing them through the eyes of Jesus and putting aside, even forgetting the circumstances of our own lives. When we "go to Jesus", our focus is right, our faith is strong.

So, what makes our faith weak? Well, it becomes clear when we look at verse 30, "But when he saw the wind boisterous, he was afraid; and beginning to sink, he cried, saying, Lord, save me." Do you see what Peter did? Actually, it's about what Peter saw. He took his eyes off

Jesus and put them back on the storm. What happens when our focus is on our circumstances? Well, like Peter, we begin to "sink" and become fearful. And, we miss the great opportunities around us to point people to Jesus. So often, we only "see" our problems and are "moved" to dwell in misery instead of dwelling in joy as the Lord desires for us. When we see the storm, our focus is wrong, our faith is weak.

Though Jesus "caught him" (v.31) and caused the wind to cease (v. 32), the last words Peter heard before reaching their next ministry stop were, "O thou of little faith, wherefore didst thou **doubt**?" (Emphasis mine).

Pray Through

"Trust in the Lord with all thine heart; and lean not unto thine own understanding. In all thy ways acknowledge him, and he shall direct thy paths." (Proverbs 3:5-6)

— □ CHAPTER 8 □ —

Fields Below, Fields Within (Window vs. Aisle)

"The harvest truly is plenteous,"
— MATTHEW 9:37 —

Growing up in the Midwest of the United States, I love fields! Corn fields, soybean fields, wheat fields, newly plowed fields, or just plain fallow fields. One of the most beautiful fields I have ever seen, though, was in Australia. It was in an area of the state of New South Wales where they grew a lot of canola. As far as the eye could see, the bright yellow flower of the canola plant just popped! It was an unbelievably beautiful sight. Pictures just don't do it justice.

I think that is my favorite part of the window seat, the fields below. I love looking down at the puzzle-like pieces, perfectly fit together. I think about the enormous harvest that comes from all of those fields, and, the number of laborers (farmers), who are needed to bring in, or harvest, all of those crops. From the window seat, those fields below seem interesting, but...

There is also the field within. Look at all of the passengers on board the plane. There must be hundreds of them. That's a pretty big field! I don't fly a lot, but I have had opportunities to talk to the person sitting next to me, even a flight attendant once, about our ministry, about salvation. But that's just one person among hundreds. What about the rest? Maybe there are some others on board sharing Jesus with the person seated next to them. I don't know. But, what if there isn't? What happens to all those people? Will they ever hear that Jesus died for their sins? It would be like a farmer, in one of the fields below, making one pass through his field and then parking his combine and saying, "Well, that's all I can do.". We'd say that is dumb! You can't do that! The crops will just wither and rot! What a waste! How sad! Do we see the field within the same way? I wonder! Do we say, with the same passion and outcry, that we can't leave those on board un-harvested? Crops left in the field die and rot. Souls left in the field spiritually die and are separated from God for all eternity in hell.

As we traveled through India, I began to understand better what Christ meant when He told His disciples, "the harvest truly is plenteous". I had only seen India from the window seat. You know, books, news, internet give one a view from a distance. But now, whoa, I'm right in the middle of the field! And it's a big field! If you have ever walked through a cornfield, and you should, everybody should, you will find the rows are narrow. You can't walk down a row without brushing against a stalk and having it hit you in the face. Much of India felt to me like walking through a cornfield (especially in the cities). This gives one a whole new perspective. It's right in your face! You see the vastness of the field. Its size is overwhelming. It causes us to act, to make a decision. Will I or won't I participate in the harvest? It's that simple, really. This is the decision you and I must make. This is the decision you and I must make right now!

In the last chapter, we looked at the events just following the amazing miracle Jesus performed in feeding the 20,000 plus people. In this chapter, I want us to take a closer look at just what took place in that field with all of those people. If you take a minute to read the account from each of the Gospel books (Matthew 14:13-21, Mark 6:31-44, Luke 9:11-17, John 6:1-13), it will help you understand the impact of this miracle.

The news had just been brought to Jesus (Being God, He would have already known) by His disciples of the beheading of John the Baptist by King Herod. Upon receiving this news, Jesus decided that He and the disciples should launch out in the boat and travel to what is described as a desert place to be away from town and the chaos. Now, I don't for one second think that Jesus was afraid of Herod coming after Him. I believe it was more likely Jesus was thinking this would be a good time to teach these fellas something valuable.

When the people in town saw Jesus and the disciples leaving, and others heard they were leaving, scripture tells us that they began heading to where Jesus was going. They still wanted to see and hear from Jesus. Though Jesus was taking the more direct route by boat, we read that when He and the disciples arrived, there was a multitude of people waiting for them. I picture thousands of people running to get to where Jesus was. They had to run to beat Him there. Pause for a minute and consider this. **When was the last time you ran to get to Jesus because you needed Him so bad?** I think too often, we sit and wait for Jesus to come to us or we just stroll along casually with no urgency to meet with Him. These people ran!

I love the plan that Jesus put in place. Imagine the chaos that was taking place in town. A beloved Prophet had just been murdered. What would that mean for those who were following Jesus, whether in faith or just out of curiosity? If they were seen hanging out with Jesus, would they be next to get their head removed? I'm sure there was fear and unrest taking place among the multitude that day. So, Jesus, knowing they would come, brought them to a place of comfort, an open place they would feel safe. Jesus removed them from the crowded chaos to a place He could now minister to them. He brought them to a place where they would truly hear His words, having their eyes, their hearts, focused on Jesus. The Bible tells us when Jesus and the disciples rolled up to shore, Jesus saw the multitude of people and, guess what, that's right, He was moved with compassion for them. It says He saw them as sheep that had no shepherd. Sound familiar? Scripture tells us, He began teaching them and healing the sick among them. Do you know what I know? People were getting saved! We see throughout the gospels the faith of people coming to Jesus, especially for physical healing, and Jesus, seeing their faith in Him, also healed them spiritually. The Bible doesn't tell us, but I just wonder if all of those people that ran to that desert place, were saved that day? I want to think so.

As the day began to drift into evening, the disciples began to worry about the people being able to get back to town in time to buy food for dinner. When they approached Jesus about this, He simply told them that the people didn't need to leave and for the disciples to just give them something to eat. Can you see the looks on their faces? Who brought that much food or any food for that matter? So the disciples assumed they needed to start the first food delivery business and go to town and bring back food for 20,000 plus people. It makes me laugh when you read in a couple of the Gospel accounts about the disciples asking Jesus if about 200 days' worth of wages (two hundred pennyworth) would be enough food to buy? Are they carrying that much money with them? They can't go to the ATM! Even if they could buy that much food, how are they going to get it there? No, let's just use what we have here was Jesus' reply. With confusion growing on the faces of the disciples, one of them speaks up and tells Jesus that all they have are five loaves and two fishes they got off of some boy. Jesus said, that'll work! Bring it to me. These guys had to be thinking, "What in the world is Jesus going to do with this?" "That's not enough for one of us." My Pastor once explained exactly what this boy's lunch would have looked like. These loaves aren't like a loaf of bread we think of. He explained that they would be baked bread about the size of a twinkie. And the fish would have been small, like sardines. Now, maybe you are starting to think, "What is Jesus going to do with this?"

Jesus has everyone sit down in this grassy field, takes the five loaves and the two fishes and then turns His eyes toward heaven. He blesses the food and thanks God for what He has provided for them. The disciples probably thought that this was really embarrassing. The people had to begin to wonder if Jesus had lost it. Jesus broke the bread and had the disciples start handing it out. What happens next is over the top remarkable. As the disciples handed out the food, it just kept coming. I mean, as you give people food to eat, you have less and less food, right? Not in this case. The Bible tells us, they ate and ate until they were full. 20,000 plus people full from five twinkies and two sardines! That is not possible! Oh, but with God, aren't all things possible? You better believe they are. Jesus even had a surprise for the disciples. After all of that hard work serving dinner to the people, it says that they took up twelve baskets full of leftovers. Twelve baskets for…twelve disciples! God always adds some cool touches to His plans, don't you think?

This was definitely what I would consider a field within. Think about it, with 20,000 plus people, the disciples would have had to each serve almost 1,700 people. That would have taken them hours. With it getting late in the day, they would have had to hurry to get all of the people served their dinner. There is no way they could have stopped to talk with, really anyone. So, why is this a problem? Well, remember, many of these people were healed by Jesus. They would have loved to talk about it. They listened to Him teach. Maybe they had questions? Some had, no doubt, put their faith in Jesus, but maybe some had not yet and just needed a little more encouraging. This was a perfect opportunity to talk with the people about who Jesus is and why they needed Him. It was a perfect time to encourage those new in their faith and to rejoice with all of those that were restored to health. The field, you could say, was huge and ready for harvest. The seeds had been planted and watered and were ready to be picked. But, how can one person, with a limited amount of time, handle 1,700 "plants"? The answer is, they can't. They needed more help to truly get the job done. Matthew 13:38a says "The field is the world…" That big a field requires a lot of workers to bring in the harvest on time. It requires the action of many. Sitting in the window seat is like the disciples handing out the food. You're there in the field, but not really accomplishing anything. Do you see the field within? Do you see how plentiful the harvest is? Or, are you stuck gazing at the field below?

Pray Through

"Call unto me, and I will answer thee, and shew thee great and mighty things, which thou knowest not." (Jeremiah 33:3)

CHAPTER 9

Fighting for the Window Seat

"but the labourers are few;"
— MATTHEW 9:37 —

As my wife and I and our two kids hopped on the plane with our YES Ministries team, heading for Grenada, a beautiful island in the West Indies, it started. I get the window seat! No! I already called it! No you didn't! Daaadddd!!!! The fight was on. Who was going to get the window seat? Who would come out the victor and who would be mad, at least until the next "important" thing arose? And why, since we were headed on a mission trip to show the love of Jesus (ironic isn't it) to others, was the window seat so important that my kids were ready to fight over it? I believe for the same reason most of us as adults fight to only "participate" in missions. What do I mean? Well, on the plane, the window seat allows you to just participate – you are along for the ride. You can stare out the window and you only have to do something when the flight attendant comes by and asks if you would like a bag of peanuts or something to drink. And even then, you can fake like you are asleep and they will pass on by you, leaving you undisturbed. Ok, so maybe I have done this! Don't judge me! But the aisle seat, that's a different story! In the aisle seat, you are involved. The flight attendants are constantly moving up and down the plane, sometimes bumping into you themselves or with the drink cart. You really have to watch your elbows! The person across the aisle starts up a conversation.

Other passengers pass by on their way to and from the restroom. The kid kicking and screaming is louder and I think he only kicks the aisle seat (though no official study has been done on this)! And the worst, just as you are finally getting comfortable and trying to settle in for a nap, the person in the window seat needs to get out to stretch their legs or go use the restroom. So, up you get! There is a difference between participating and being involved. So, how does that look concerning missions, participation versus involvement?

Now, I will preface my explanation with this. Participation and involvement are good, but I believe the problem in most churches and with the majority of Christians today is that we have settled for participation and use it to justify our non-involvement. Settled! Actually, our participation should be our entrance to and affect our involvement in the Great Commission. That is what God has shown and dealt with me about for years. I love missions and thought I always had. I gave money to missions (a good thing). I have bought dinners for missionaries who were visiting (a good thing). I have attended churches that have missions programs (a good thing). I get really excited when missionaries talk about what God is doing through their ministry (a good thing). But something is missing, something very important. Involvement! That's where the love for missions comes from - being involved. Let me see if I can paint a picture to explain.

Why get involved? Because that is exactly what God told us to do. GO! (read Matthew 28:19 and Mark 16:15). Not WATCH! I love missions because I am involved in what God loves. His Son Jesus is the core of the entire message of missions. Yes, I may have the opportunity to help send someone to the mission field. Yes, I may have the opportunity to pray for a missionary or a mission team. All of those things are good and needed, but it does not mean we are involved. Don't miss the importance of getting on the plane, or the bus, or van, or car, or whatever the vehicle which gets you to the field to join the harvest. I tell the teams we have had the pleasure of leading on mission trips, I am proud of them for getting on the plane. Why would I say that? Because for the 10-20 people who get on the plane, make the commitment, obey the Lord's command, three times that many tell me they are interested, but…

- *"I don't have that much money."* 9 out of 10 people who have taken part in our mission trips cannot write a check for the total amount. They have to raise their funds, which takes work! We have had 70+ year old folks with fixed incomes raise every penny by selling pizzas and through the donations of others. We have had 12 year old kids who have taken on babysitting jobs, sold pizzas, and written letters to friends and family in order to raise the funds needed.
- *"I've never been out of the country before."* Ok!
- *"I'm afraid of flying."* We had a 50+ year old man on our last trip to Grenada who was absolutely terrified to fly (he never had before). God used him greatly and I know he would get on a plane again a million times to be involved in The Great Commission.
- *"I don't have time/can't get off work."* But, they have their 1-2-3 weeks of vacation already planned for the year.
- And, my favorite (rant about to ensue), *"I don't feel the Lord is leading me to go."* At this point, I politely excuse myself from the conversation while inside I come unglued (just being honest). **You have got to be absolutely kidding me! That's the excuse you are giving me? Please, please, please, just be honest and tell me you don't want to go! Please just tell me it is because you just don't want to give up your vacation time! Please just tell me it's not that important to you! But don't ever tell me it's because God is not "leading" you to go! God is telling you NOT to go tell people about His Son Jesus? The Great Commission is for everyone but you? God has given you a GET OUT pass for "Go ye into all the world"? Give me a break! The harvest is plenteous, it's HUGE and the labourers are few! There aren't enough people going into the harvest! That means crops (souls) will die and enter an eternal hell and God's not "leading" you to go!**

I was speaking at a church in our area one Sunday night. I told the congregation though Missionaries are happy to receive money, clothing, food, supplies (participation), what they get real excited about is that person who comes and serves side by side with them, right there in the dirt of the field (involvement). In attendance that night was a young man who was on deputation, raising support to go to the mission field of Mexico. His parents, who I went to church with years ago, are currently Missionaries in Mexico. So, this young man had grown up understanding missions and the missionary life. After the service, he came up to me and said, *"You are exactly right. It's such a blessing and so encouraging when people come."* Don't fight for the window seat. If you are going to fight, fight to be in the aisle seat. God is leading you to go. Get involved! Be a part of the boots on the ground. It is the most amazing and powerful thing you will ever experience.

The Jews and the Samaritans didn't like each other - which is an understatement. The Jews saw the Samaritans as dogs, less than dogs probably. If a Jew had to travel and Samaria was between them and where they were going, they would literally walk around Samaria, even though it meant their journey would be significantly longer, just to keep from having to interact with the Samaritan people. I think it would be safe to say that there were not enough "missionaries" serving in Samaria for the sake of the Gospel. It is where we find ourselves in the Gospel of John 4:3-45.

Scripture tells us, just as John the Baptist was, that Jesus had been going around making and baptizing disciples (His 12 disciples doing the baptizing). To no surprise, this made the "religious" leaders, the Pharisees, unhappy. Of course, everything Jesus did made the "religious" leaders unhappy! I think we are seeing that same attitude, just with a different look, in the American church today. My guess is, most people really didn't like the Pharisees. They came across proud, arrogant, cranky and "better than thou". They came across this way because that is exactly how they were. Many of today's "religious" leaders come across excited, humble, loving and welcoming. You might say, but, isn't that the way we are supposed to be? Isn't that how Jesus was? Yes and No. Yes, we should have these characteristics genuinely on display in our lives, no doubt about it. But, the No is, they have to match up with scripture. What do I mean? Many in the American church believe that the Bible isn't relevant in our culture today. By that, I mean there are people who believe some of the teachings in the Bible do not apply in today's culture and we need to look at them in a different way. I won't re-hash this thought (go back and read chapter 2 on this subject), but the question is, how can we actually live out the character of Jesus but not completely follow His teachings? If I may challenge believers, please don't work on being religious, but work on your relationship with Jesus. The best way to do this? Become a "labourer" in the field for Christ.

Now, back to Samaria! Jesus decides that it is time to head back to Galilee and He informs the disciples that it is a necessity that they pass through Samaria and not travel around it. We don't know how the disciples responded to this, but we can guess that they weren't really excited about going to Samaria. Jesus arrives first, by Himself, in the city of Sychar. This was near a piece of land that Jacob gave to his son Joseph and where Jacob's well was located. That is actually where Jesus showed up to right at midday. A perfect spot, at the heat of the day, for a wearied traveler. The problem is that Jesus didn't have any way of drawing water from the well and no one came to the well at this time of day. It was just too hot. Wait, Jesus was in luck (not really)! A woman just happened (not really) to show up to the well and to get water. No, she was the necessity that Jesus gave as the reason He needed to go through Samaria. Why? Why her? Why was she there at this time of day? We'll see why shortly.

Jesus starts off the conversation with this Samaritan woman by asking her to give Him a drink of water. This would have been an odd request and the woman picked up on that right away. She immediately asks why Jesus, being a Jew, would ask her, a Samaritan woman, for a drink and then, as if to remind Him, says, "for the Jews have no dealings with the Samaritans." (John 4:9). In that culture, there was a whole lot wrong with this conversation.

"Jesus answered and said unto her, If thou knewest the gift of God, and who it is that saith to thee, Give me to drink; thou wouldest have asked of him, and he would have given thee living water." (John 4:10). Like most, she has no idea at this point what Jesus is talking about. We see it in her response back to Him. The well is deep and you don't have anything to draw water with. Jacob, who she refers to as their father, put this well in and is highly revered and she questions if Jesus is actually saying that He is greater than Jacob? Surely that's not what He is saying? Jesus continues to give her a little more information by comparing the water from the well and the "living water" He is offering. Jesus tells her that anyone who drinks the water from the well will have to come back to it again and again because it will only satisfy their thirst for a short time. The "living water", Jesus explains, is like having your own built-in well right inside you. It never runs out and so you never will thirst again. Don't you love the woman's response in verse 15? She said, "...Sir, give me this water, that I thirst not, neither come hither to draw." Absolutely! I'll take some! Who wouldn't want to never be thirsty again? The second reason she gives for wanting the "living water" is interesting, though. What's the big deal about coming to the well to get water? Why would that be a big plus for this woman? We are about to see why.

With the woman not quite getting it (like we would have), Jesus takes the conversation in a different direction. He hits a little closer to home, if you will, to help her understand. He tells the woman to go get her husband and bring him back with her. A simple and reasonable request, I suppose. The woman immediately responds that she doesn't have a husband. I can see her jaw hit the ground, when Jesus said, 'You're right!" "You've actually had five husbands and the dude you are living with now isn't your husband." Ahh, she thinks! Now I get it, you are a prophet. The conversation continues with a discussion of where to worship and how to worship and when Jesus finishes, the woman tells Him what she has been taught all her life. "The woman saith unto him, I know that Messias cometh, which is called Christ: when he is come, he will tell us all things." (v. 25). Get ready! The light bulb is about to come on. "Jesus saith unto her, I that speak unto thee am he." (v. 26). BAM! She gets it. This is the Messiah! And, by the looks of it, she believed. Jesus, the labourer in the field of Samaria, has

His first convert and she doesn't wait to be taught for a year or two or twenty to get to work doing her calling (and our calling), telling people about and bringing people to Jesus. Did you realize you are equipped and prepared to share Christ with others the moment you get saved? Well, you are! This is an excuse many use for not getting into the field and laboring, I'm not equipped, I'm not knowledgeable enough, I'm just not ready. Wrong!

It was at this point, that the disciples were returning from buying meat in town. They were amazed that Jesus was talking to this woman, but no one said anything. Why would they be amazed? Well, first, just the fact that a Jewish man was talking with a Samaritan woman was frowned upon and especially talking with her one on one, alone. Second, because of the time of day. Women didn't come to get water in the heat of the day, unless they were women of ill-repute. She may have been a prostitute or and least a woman that was known for being promiscuous. She had to come to the well at that time of day because no one wanted to be around her or have her around. Among a people who were viewed as dogs by the Jews, she was below that. That's pretty low.

As the disciples walked up, the woman was dropping her water pot and running off to town to share the news she had just received. Who was she going to tell, though? No one wanted to be around her or talk with her. But, that didn't stop her. She ran up to a group of men and told them that they had to come meet this guy that told her everything she has done in her life. As I'm sure the men just looked at her like she was a lunatic, she asks the question to them, "is not this the Christ? Attention grabbed! They immediately headed toward the well to meet this Jesus and see what He was all about.

As the crowd was approaching, Jesus was still teaching, just a different lesson, this time to His disciples. Jesus never missed an opportunity to grow someone spiritually. The disciples were trying to get Jesus to eat some meat, but Jesus' response was that His meat was to do the will of His Father. You know Peter was thinking, "Why can't Jesus just ever explain something plainly?" What does that mean? Had someone already fed Him? We don't understand! Pointing to the crowd approaching, Jesus tells the disciples that they think although the harvest time is four months away, the field is ready to be picked now. Get ready boys! You may not have sown the seeds, but you can help water and bring in the harvest. You will be paid wages and pick fruit that are eternal. I love how God works in the lives of others. The Samaritan woman, saved only a matter of minutes, is already producing fruit, "And many of the Samaritans of that city believed on him for the saying of the woman," (v. 39). That is what faith coupled with action will result in. Jesus' short-term mission trip was a powerful two-day trip. Only two days! As He taught, "many more believed because of his own word;" (v. 41). Still not sure? Just do what the Samaritan woman did, bring them to Jesus and let Him do the rest, *"Now we believe...for we have heard him ourselves, and know that this is indeed the Christ, the Saviour of the world."* (v. 42) (**Emphasis mine**).

With the Jews attitude toward the Samaritans being as it was, they would walk added miles and hours around Samaria just so they didn't come into contact with Samaritans. Who is reaching these people for Christ? Isn't that Jesus' point? Samaria is a field with a large harvest to be had and nobody is going there. No Jew at least. At least not until Jesus took a two-day short term mission trip there. You see, taking part in the harvest doesn't mean you will have to move to _____ (insert the place you'd be afraid God would call you too). Jesus didn't stay in Samaria for good, but He did have a great impact on them while He was there. Why hadn't anybody taken this opportunity? Oh, I know what it is, the Lord hasn't led anyone to go, right? This scripture is one that convicts and breaks my heart the most. What this chapter's scripture tells me is there are a lot of people who will die and spend eternity in hell only because there were not enough people (and I am to blame at times too) willing to "go". You and I may not solve the problem of too few "labourers" completely, but if we will commit our lives to go for Jesus, just like the Samaritan woman did, souls will be saved and, most importantly, God will be pleased. What do you say? Will you keep fighting for the window seat or will you join the harvest, wherever that may be, and fight for the aisle?

Pray Through

"I am debtor both to the Greeks, and to the Barbarians; both to the wise, and to the unwise. So, as much as in me is, I am ready to preach the gospel to you that are at Rome also. For I am not ashamed of the gospel of Christ: for it is the power of God unto salvation to every one that believeth; to the Jew first, and also to the Greek." (Romans 1:14-16)

CHAPTER 10

Consider Where You Sit – Grace After School Clubs

"Pray ye therefore the Lord of the harvest,"
— MATTHEW 9:38 —

Where you "sit" in ministry is important. Now, I don't mean sit like in a recliner, but rather where you serve, where you are involved. As you can guess from our portion of scripture highlighting this chapter, the most important thing you can do when determining where to "sit" is pray.

My friend Peter and I began praying for our India trip long before we stepped foot on the airplane. In fact, I had been praying about the Lord's will for YES Ministries in India some two years before I mentioned it to Peter and asked him to pray about the possibility of accompanying me on the trip. As we began putting our plans together, we prayed about many things. We prayed about when to go and how long we should stay. We prayed about which ministries to visit while there. We prayed God would show us where He wanted us involved, if He indeed wanted us involved in India. We were willing to go just to proclaim the gospel, if that was what God wanted us to do. We prayed about raising the finances we needed. We prayed for each other, that God would speak to us and He would use us to be a blessing and an encouragement to those we met in India. We prayed for protection. The devil really tried to use fear on me as a deterrent. We prayed for wisdom. We prayed for God's direction about YES Ministries' involvement in India. We prayed that God would stamp it on my heart and direct me to where that involvement should be. He did just that through the Grace After School Clubs.

I prayed that if there was an area of ministry God would have us involved in, that it would truly connect with the heart of YES Ministries. We want to see youth come to know Christ as Savior, be discipled, and grow into strong witnesses and disciple makers of Jesus. The first day in Hyderabad, we spoke at several churches, visited a slum, and met with several local Pastors. All of this was encouraging, heartbreaking, challenging, but no stamp. Speaking in churches is something I am thankful we get to do wherever we are ministering. Though the goal in the slum area is to share the gospel, there is a heavy focus on meeting social needs for men, women, and children. Again, a great need with the right goal in mind, but as I've learned, though you desperately want to, you can't do everything. What encourages your heart is knowing God has just the right person for the job. I pray they step up and accept the challenge. And, in the third case, God has not called me to Pastoral care, though I believe He used Peter and me that first day to encourage and challenge the Pastors we met with.

As I mentioned in Chapter 7, that first night God revealed to us His change in our plans. Or, probably better put, decided we hadn't listened closely enough to what His plan was for us. One of the changes we made was to spend more time with Pastor Wilson. He was a tremendous blessing and was truly the key to our understanding the impact of the various ministries that we visited. His help, especially in the area of communication, was vital. Because there are so many different languages and dialects throughout India, there were times when Peter, a native of India, also needed translation. You can only imagine how in the dark I was! The extra time we had with Pastor Wilson allowed me to share more of our vision at YES Ministries. More importantly for me, it was time to better get a sense of his heart and his ministry. Some of the questions and concerns we had prior to arriving in India were well answered during our time spent with Pastor Wilson and, may I add, his wonderful family. God was preparing our heart for His stamp. That stamp came Tuesday evening, October 7, 2014.

When Peter got sick, it forced us to cancel our second day with Pastor Wilson. Our plan was to spend two full days with each of the three ministries we had on our schedule. It doesn't seem like much, but with travel and a very tight budget, it was all we could do. In that ten day stretch, we didn't have much breathing room and definitely didn't have time for changes to our schedule. But, again, that was our plan. God had a different plan.

Peter and I spent all day Monday at the hotel. That was tough, especially on Peter. I know he felt like he messed things up, but that proved to be far from the truth. It's hard to see that when you are in the midst of the plan. We both were absolutely whooped! Peter from being up all night sick and me from being up all night and my body trying to figure out where it was, when it was to sleep, and when it was supposed to be up. It was a mess! Though we both struggled, feeling like we were wasting a day, I believe wisdom prevailed. If we would have pushed ourselves to keep the schedule we planned, I think it could have been devastating. We needed rest and so that is what we did. We spent the day just relaxing at the hotel, communicating with the other ministries and Pastor Wilson, re-adjusting our schedule.

We finally agreed on the changes we needed to make. We would spend Tuesday, the day we were scheduled to travel to Bhadrachalam, in Hyderabad with Pastor Wilson and visit one of their Grace After School Clubs. On Wednesday, Pastor Wilson would drive us the eight hours to Bhadrachalam to meet with the RTM Team. They do work in the remote tribal areas. Originally, he was not going to travel with us, but oh what a blessing it turned out to be having him with us. Can I stop for a second and say something? You need to write this down. It's deep and profound. Ready? **God knows what He is doing!** Wednesday evening we visited their orphanage home. Thursday, we spent all day with the RTM Team visiting several remote tribal areas. Friday, it was back to Hyderabad. The third ministry on our schedule, we had to cancel altogether. Though we hated to do it, it definitely worked out for the best. God protected us, not from any danger that I know of, but from becoming involved in a situation not suited for our ministries vision. We praise the Lord for His protective hand.

Back to Tuesday, October 7th. Since we weren't scheduled to be in Hyderabad, Peter and I remained at the hotel for the morning while Pastor Wilson took care of some of his ministry duties. As the morning went on, I was thankful that Peter was feeling much better. In fact, he suggested we go for a walk and get some fresh air (which, as much as I enjoyed India, I would have to say is a bit of a stretch, especially in the cities). What we didn't know was God was not done, let's say, helping us understand His change in plans. Unfortunately for my friend Peter, he was the vessel by which we would learn. As we walked along the edge of the street, I heard Peter groan. When I looked back, he was behind me. It appeared he had caught himself from falling down, but that he had done something that caused him some pain. I looked to see if he had stepped in a pothole or tripped over something, but it was just the slight down-slope from the sidewalk to the street that caused him to roll his ankle. He seemed ok, but we would find out later, that was not the case. One thing we would do on this trip is walk a lot and we would quickly realize there were not many smooth, flat surfaces in India.

We headed out that afternoon with Pastor Wilson. We were excited about visiting the after school clubs. My involvement The Great Adventure Club, a after school club at home, added interest and excitement to the visit. As we made our way across town, Pastor Wilson shared more with us about the clubs, what we could expect, and what his goals are for the clubs in Hyderabad. As of our visit, there were currently eight clubs meeting. Pastor Wilson's goal is to have forty clubs meeting throughout Hyderabad. Each club has 15-30 kids attending. If a club hits the thirty kid mark, another club will be started in that area. So, there is potential for lots of clubs to be started. The draw for the families whose kids attend one of the Grace clubs is the assistance the kids get with their schoolwork. Each club has an on-site teacher for this purpose. Because these clubs are held in very poor, predominantly slum areas, the chance for education is so important. Parents hold to the view that it is really the only chance for their kids to have a "better" life. That is why there are kids from all different backgrounds, including Hindu and Muslim families. Don't forget, the ultimate goal of the Grace Clubs is to teach the kids about Jesus Christ. This is accomplished by teaching them, during club time, about Christ through songs and Bible accounts. Each kid is also required, as part of the program, to memorize scripture verses each week. The non-Christian families know this, but still send their kids because they get help with their schooling. That is so Awesome! As Pastor Wilson explained this to us, I'm telling you, I was getting pumped! I thought, "This is what I'm looking for!" I know there is a social aspect to the Grace clubs, but they do not stop there. Most groups in India focus on meeting the social and physical needs - important, but only temporary. With Grace Clubs, meeting the social need (temporary) is simply the avenue to the Gospel, meeting the spiritual need (eternal). I can't wait to get to the club!

I shared this food cart moment in chapter 5, but wanted to paint the picture again of this place where God would have us "sit". We came to a stop alongside the road. Pastor Wilson showed us the entrance to the slum where the club we were visiting meets. We waited for the Pastor of the church where the club meets. He would lead us to the club. Why? Well, as Pastor Wilson explained, though he has visited this club many times, he still can't remember how to get to it. I had no idea what I was about to witness! The local Pastor pulled up on his motorcycle and dropped off a young girl, his daughter, who I guessed to be about ten years old. He said she would lead the way and off he went. And then off she went! And, so, off we went, into what seemed like a whole other world. We began to wind our way through the streets, wide enough only for foot traffic and motorcycles or bicycles. I didn't take me long to understand why Pastor Wilson had a hard time remembering how to get to the club. It was so narrow, with the homes (1 or 2 rooms is all) crammed so tightly together, you couldn't get a sense of where you were. I picture someone looking over from above us saying, "Turn left. Go straight. No, no, right, go right! Come back! Left, left!"

As with the whole trip, I loved the looks on the faces of the kids when I walked into the church (again just 1 small room) where this particular club meets. Some immediately smile, as I'm smiling at all of them, while others just stare (and who can blame them)! We listened as the kids sang about Jesus and quoted their scripture verses. I shared with them and challenged them to follow Jesus. We watched as they did their schoolwork. I saw Pastor Wilson's heart as he interacted with the kids and how they responded to him. It was exactly what we came to India to see, the ministry itself and the heart behind the ministry. As the week went on, we continued to pray about the areas of ministry we were seeing. We continued to consider where we would "sit". Our minds kept going back to the Grace After School Clubs. I felt that they were the one ministry that truly connected with our ministry. God reminded me, you want to reach kids, you want to disciple kids, you want to help send kids, this is where you can do just those things. As we sat with Pastor Wilson for the last time, I shared with him that YES Ministries wanted to be involved with the Grace After School Clubs. We gave him a commitment and the financial support to begin five more clubs, beginning in January 2015. We believe God has put his stamp on it. What about you? Have you considered where you will "sit"? *"Pray ye therefore the Lord of the harvest"*. He will put you in the right seat.

Two things you absolutely must do when you consider where you will "sit" is, 1) Put it to prayer and 2) Count the cost. Don't see these two things as the "right" Bible answers (in word only), but as answers the Bible says are right (action).

Prayer is defined simply as *a request of God*. You are requesting of God to guide you and to put within you His passion for His work that He wants you to do. If you want to have great clarity as to where God wants you to "sit", you have to know and put to practice, three Spirit moving words. You can find these words in 1 Thessalonians 5:17, "Pray without ceasing." You have to be constantly before the Lord. The second part of James 5:16 says, "The effectual (**unceasing**) fervent prayer of a righteous man availeth much." As we look at this area of prayer, let's start by agreeing on this one thing…Prayer Works!

I believe prayer is such a vital part of this process, but, it's not about what I think, so, in this section, we are going to look at what God thinks about prayer. We've already said that God believes we should be constantly praying because it works. Let's look at what God says about 1) Who should be included in our prayers, 2) What to include in our prayers, and 3) How to approach our prayers.

Who should be included in your prayer to see where you should "sit"? First, you should be involved. I know, duh! But, wait, don't just dismiss this as a dumb comment. The idea of where God wants you to "sit" is a personal thing between you and God and, too often, we don't spend enough time talking to God about it. We either sit and wait on Him or we only trust the prayers of others to bring an answer. We will look at the importance of including others in our prayer, but do not miss the opportunity or responsibility that you and I have in seeing God place us in that perfect place to do His perfect work that has a perfect result. So, what does our part look like? Matthew 6:6 tells us, "But thou, when thou prayest, enter into thy closet, and when thou hast shut thy door, pray to thy Father which is in secret; and thy Father which seeth thee in secret shall reward thee openly." Spend time alone with God, just you and God and make your prayer closet a place without distractions.

Second, include your family in praying for this. Remember, it will affect their lives as well and they love you and want to see God use your life for His glory. There is a man in Acts 10 named Cornelius. It says in verse 2 that Cornelius was "A devout man, and one that feared God with **all his house**, which gave much alms to the people, and prayed to God always." (Emphasis mine). Cornelius made God and prayer a part of his family time and because he involved his family in praying for important matters, verse 31 tells us, "thy prayer is heard". Family is great for getting the ear of God.

Third, include your friends or peer groups. Do you belong to a men's or ladie's group or are you in a small group at your church? If you're a teen, include your youth group or your team. Maybe you sit on a Board of Directors or are in a card club. I don't know! Involve those outside your family whom you trust to pray on your behalf. "For where two or three are gathered together in my name, there am I in the midst of them." (Matthew 18:20). It only takes a few, praying in unity, and God is smack dab in the middle of it (where you want Him to be)!

So, now we are praying about where to "sit" and we've brought in some reinforcements through friends and family, what do we include in these prayers? Well, we pray in JOY. What is JOY you ask? It is an acronym that stands for Jesus, Others, You. That is how we are supposed to pray. You may be thinking, if I am asking God what He wants me to do, why am I praying for myself last? Not to sound mean, but why am I praying for others now? That's a good question. We'll talk about that in a minute. Remember the "J"? First, our prayers must focus on Jesus. This would be considered a prayer of adoration. In Daniel chapter 4, we see King Nebuchadnezzar getting a little too big for his britches and let's just say that God cuts him down to size. Because he had built a vast kingdom, King Neb thought he was something special. The Bible says that God drove him out and made him eat grass like the oxen. He literally became a beast in the field. The Bible tells us that his hair grew like eagles' feathers and his nails like birds' claws and he lived in that condition for seven years. Then one day he looked toward heaven and scripture says that his *"understanding"*, or reasoning, came back to him. This is when the king, who thought he was something, said this about the King of Kings, "and I blessed the most High, and I praised and honoured him that liveth for ever, whose dominion is an everlasting dominion, and his kingdom is from generation to generation: And all the inhabitants of the earth are reputed as nothing: and he doeth according to his will in the army of heaven, and among the inhabitants of the earth: and none can stay his hand, or say unto him, What doest thou?" (Daniel 4:34, 35). That, my friends, is adoration. Do your prayers start off with how much you adore Jesus? They should!

Second, in praying JOY, is our prayers for others. Praying on behalf of others is called intercessory prayer. Praying for others, you might say, unleashes the power of God's will in our own life. Does it really matter that much? It sure does! Why? It matters because God's word tells us that He wants us to think of others before ourselves. Philippians 2:3a-4 tells us this, "but in lowliness of mind let each esteem other better than themselves. Look not every man on his own things, but every man also on the things of others." It's really cool how God blesses us more, the more we put others first. That seems like a good idea when we are looking for the blessings of God's will. James 5:14, 15 tells us that one of the best ways we can pray for others is when they are sick. Sickness is a constant in a fallen world and many of us have dealt with friends or family suffering from a common cold to cancer. God tells us through James that our prayers can lead to the healing of someone. That's not to pat ourselves on the back as if we have some great power, but that through faithful prayer, we can see a great God unleash His power.

Third, we reach ourselves. This is when I start praying for all the things I want, right? Well, not exactly! In the next section, we'll consider more about how we approach prayer for ourselves. But here, our focus is on making sure our relationship with God has nothing hindering it. The thing that hinders or strains our relationship with God is sin. So, we need to pray, confessing our sin. 1 John 1:9 says, "If we confess our sins, he (**God**) is faithful and just to forgive us our sins, and to cleanse us from all unrighteousness." If we do our part, look at all that Jesus does. He forgives us and He cleans us up to make us able to get back in the work He has called us to. Think about that for a second. Jesus Christ died for our sins, knowing that, even as believers, you and I would still sin. So, when we pray the prayer of confession, Jesus, the Son, reminds the Father that He (Jesus) has already paid for that sin and that the payment was acceptable to the Father. Ephesians 1:7 tells us, "In whom we have redemption through his blood, the forgiveness of sins, according to the riches of his grace;". So, the Father agrees with the forgiveness given to us and now sees us as "clean" as Jesus is, which is perfect righteousness. That is unbelievable that God would see us as He sees His Son, Jesus. Are you seeing now how much God wants to answer your prayers with power? When He sees you through Jesus, He gets excited! I like it when God is excited with me. That thought excites me with anticipation about what God is going to do through me. I hope it excites you as well.

The glue that holds all these prayers together and gives them tremendous strength is our thanksgiving. "Be careful for nothing: but in every thing by prayer and supplication with thanksgiving let your requests be made known unto God." (Philippians 4:6). God tells us not to worry about anything. That's why we're usually praying isn't it, because we are worried about something. But God says to take that worry and pray about it, to ask God to answer our prayer and to do so with a thankful heart. When we do that, we keep the focus on God and not our concern or circumstance, which gives us peace and comfort when we need it most, "And the peace of God, which passeth all understanding, shall keep your hearts and minds through Christ Jesus." (Philippians 4:7). Thank you Lord!

The other thing we said you must do when considering where you will "sit" in ministry is Count the Cost. Though you should absolutely get into the harvest right away, you need to also understand what it means to be in the Gospel harvest. There is a cost, but the cost to us pales in comparison to what Jesus paid for our sins. Don't forget that. Too many Christians respond like the rich young ruler (who I don't believe was saved) did when Jesus tells him what it will cost to follow Him. He walked away angry. His attitude was, Jesus was asking too much of him. Jesus wanted him to recognize who He was, the Messiah, as we are to recognize what He did, as Savior. It is absurd for a Christian to respond that same way. I'm not saying we don't fail at this at times, but if that is our attitude overall, we really need to do a heart check to see if we are really saved. The cost is spelled out in Luke 9:23, "And he said to them all, if any man will come after me, let him deny himself, and take up his cross daily, and follow me." How many people did God tell that this was the requirement to follow Jesus? ALL! And, what are the requirements? The first is we have to deny ourselves. That just means what I want doesn't matter. It's all about what Jesus wants. The cool thing is, when we truly deny ourselves, what we want is what God wants. So, following Jesus gives me exactly what I want because I share His heart. The next thing we have to do is take up our cross. The cross was an instrument of torture and death. Whoa! What is God asking of us? Well, a dead person doesn't have a say in anything. I don't mean to sound harsh, but it's true. Our mindset and our actions have to say, I'm not in control of my life, I don't have a say. And, this mindset must be renewed "daily". I am going to save the last thing we have to do when counting the cost until the end of the chapter.

When it comes to our prayers, how does God want us to approach them?

1. With Simplicity – "And when thou prayest, thou shalt not be as the hypocrites are: for they love to pray standing in the synagogues and in the corners of the streets, that they may be seen of men. Verily I say unto you, They have their reward. But Thou, when thou prayest, enter into thy closet, and when thou hast shut thy door, pray to thy Father which is in secret; and thy Father which seeth in secret shall reward thee openly." (Matthew 6:5, 6).

2. With Humility and Repentance – "Two men went up into the temple to pray; the one a Pharisee, and the other a publican. The Pharisee stood and prayed thus with himself, God, I thank thee, that I am not as other men are, extortioners, unjust, adulterers, or even as this publican. I fast twice in the week, I give tithes of all that I possess. And the publican, standing afar off, would not lift up so much as his eyes unto heaven, but smote upon his breast, saying, God be merciful to me a sinner. I tell you, this man went down to his house justified rather than the other: for every one that exalteth himself shall be abased; and he that humbleth himself shall be exalted." (Luke 18:10-14).

3. With Intensity – "that men ought always to pray, and not to faint;" (Luke 18:1). "Ask, and it shall be given you; seek, and ye shall find; knock, and it shall be opened unto you: For every one that asketh receiveth; and he that seeketh findeth; and to him that knocketh it shall be opened." (Matthew 7:7, 8).

4. With Confident Expectation – "Therefore I say unto you, What things soever ye desire, when ye pray, believe that ye receive them, and ye shall have them." (Mark 11:24).

I said we would finish with the last step of counting the cost. The final thing we have to do, when counting the cost, is actually follow Jesus. That means He leads. If Jesus decides to go somewhere I don't like, too bad. I follow! If Jesus decides it's time to go at 3:00 a.m., I follow! If Jesus decides to travel by foot (meaning the hard way), I follow! Where, when and how Jesus leads, I follow! No questions, no complaining. Are you ready to consider where you will "sit"? Pray to the Lord of the harvest. He has the perfect place for you.

Pray Through

"And thine ears shall hear a word behind thee, saying, This is the way, walk ye in it, when ye turn to the right hand, and when ye turn to the left." (Isaiah 30:21)

CHAPTER 11

Book Your Ticket

"that he will send forth labourers"
— MATTHEW 9:38 —

I sat in the office of my friend Peter. I had shared with him on several occasions the conversations I had with the ministries in India over the past couple of years. We had discussed my desire to visit them and see their ministries firsthand. I believe God had laid that on my heart. I had asked Peter to pray about going with me. Being a native of India and still having family there, I just felt Peter would be a great asset. And, he was for sure. As we sat in his office, he expressed to me that he would love to take part in the trip. That was all I needed to hear. Knowing his heart, just wanting to help our ministry, there was only one thing left to say…Book the tickets!

Now, we had visited the ministries we wanted to see. We had spent quality time with their leaders and saw firsthand the different aspects and areas of their ministries. We talked about the staggering feeling that gripped us when we looked upon the living conditions in the slums. We spoke of the joy of seeing the faces of the children at a local orphanage as we dished out meals to them. We stood in awe of the beauty of God's creation in the remote forest areas where small tribal villages were carved out. But it was the ministry of The Grace After School Clubs that really grabbed my heart. The thought of helping them with their education, and meeting that need, while having the opportunity to introduce kids of various religions to Jesus, the One and Only True God and Savior, that caused me to say, "Let's book our ticket". This is the area of God's harvest that He wants us to work in. How do I know? We did what Jesus told us to do, PRAY! Pray that the Lord will send forth labourers. We prayed, He sent…He sent us!

If you continue on from our text in Matthew 9 to chapter 10, you will find that it was the disciples, who Jesus told to pray for labourers, who became the labourers. Jesus sent them. When you pray the way we discussed in the last chapter, you will see that you begin to have the desire to be one of God's labourers, making it possible for Him to then call you into the labor He has prepared for you. We think if we pray like Jesus asks us to that He will surely pick someone else to go. But He wants you and me. Our Creator, our Saviour, wants you and me. How do we say no to Him? Sadly, all too often, we do so very easily it seems.

What God desires is that you and I will yield our lives to Him. What exactly does that mean? Yielded is defined as, "to give up or surrender (oneself), as to a superior power or authority". So, God is asking us to surrender ourselves to His authority in our life. Romans 6:13 says, "Neither yield ye your members as instruments of unrighteousness unto sin: but yield yourselves unto God, as those that are alive from the dead, and your members as instruments of righteousness unto God." James 4:7 tells us, "Submit yourselves therefore to God. Resist the devil, and he will flee from you." So, what exactly are we yielding to God? First, we are to yield our bodies, "I beseech you therefore, brethren, by the mercies of God, that ye present your bodies a living sacrifice, holy, acceptable unto God, which is your reasonable service." (Romans 12:1). 1 Corinthians 6:20 says, "For ye are bought with a price: therefore glorify God in your body, and in your spirit, which are God's." When Jesus died on the cross for our sins, He purchased us. That is why these verses tell us our body is to be yielded, or surrendered, to God, because it belongs to Him. Second, we are to yield our minds, "And be not conformed to this world: but be ye transformed by the renewing of your mind, that ye may prove what is that good, and acceptable, and perfect, will of God." (Romans 12:2). Think about it this way. Our mind conceives or formulates the actions and our body carries it out.

That is why it is vital that our whole being is presented to God for His service. It can't just be the body and not the mind or the mind and not the body, it has to be both together. Yielding our body and mind to God is not saying that I am willing to do a specific thing and that only. No, it is when you or I dedicate them (our lives) to do whatever God commands.

Yielding can and should result in separation. Separation from what? Romans 12:2 told us, "And be not conformed to this world". We are to be separated from the world. What do we mean? The Bible tells us that the world is opposed to God. Whatever God stands for, the world is against. Whatever God is against, the world is for. Wouldn't you agree with that assessment? So, since the world is opposed to God, we as Christians then can't revel (enjoy) in the lusts of the world and still think that we can do God's will. Look at 1 John 2:15-17, "Love not the world, neither the things that are in the world. If any man love the world, the love of the Father is not in him. For all that is in the world, the lust of the flesh, and the lust of the eyes, and the pride of life, is not of the Father, but is of the world. And the world passeth away, and the lust thereof: but he that doeth the will of God abideth for ever." Jesus tells us that if we love this world and the things in it, then we are not saved. We can only have one true love and God demands that it be Him. Don't forget, He purchased you from an eternal hell if you have trusted by faith in Jesus, His Son. It is not too much for Him to ask this of us.

The word "conformed" is translated "fashioning" in 1 Peter 1:14, "As obedient children, not *fashioning* yourselves according to the former lusts in your ignorance:" (Emphasis mine). Remember your teen years (maybe you are there now). Remember the brands that were popular and everybody wanted, maybe jeans or a certain shoe. Maybe it was a hairstyle or just a certain look or style. What was that all about? Why did we want to be fashionable? It all comes down to wanting to fit in. Isn't it a little funny and a lot sad that, to fit in, we were willing to look like, talk like, and act like the group we wanted to be part of? I know the terminology has changed, but if you were a teen of the 1980's, you knew who the jocks were, the preps, the hoods, just by what they wore, how they talked, or how they acted. God tells us that if we are going to yield to Him our lives, we are to be unfashionable. We are to be unfashionable in spirit, thought, values, and actions according to the world's standards.

I want to go back for a minute to the yielding of our mind. When we yield our mind, it requires there be a transformation of it. A transformation is a thorough or dramatic change in form or appearance. Our mind needs to be thoroughly and dramatically changed and this can only be accomplished through a lifetime of "renewing" the mind. Our mind needs to be renewed because it has been darkened by sin. Romans 8:7 tells us, "Because the carnal mind is enmity against God; for it is not subject to the law of God, neither indeed can be." Also, Colossians 1:21 says, "And you, that were sometime alienated and enemies in your mind by wicked works, yet now hath he reconciled." We must be brought to the place of thinking like God thinks, "And be renewed in the spirit of your mind." (Ephesians 4:23). Our mind must be made new. This renewing comes through practicing two important things. First, we are to make it a practice of praying to God for everything. Philippians 4:6, 7 reminds us this, "Be careful for nothing; but in every thing by prayer and supplication with thanksgiving let your requests be made known unto God. And the peace of God, which passeth all understanding, shall keep your hearts and minds through Christ Jesus." Second, we need to practice constant meditation on the Word of God, "Blessed are the undefiled in the way, who walk in the law of the Lord." (Psalm 119:1). You could actually read the entirety of Psalm 119 to get a good idea of the sense of power, authority, and influence God gives His Word.

This transformation process will not be complete until we are with Christ in heaven. Two verses give us such great hope of this. Philippians 1:6 says, "Being confident of this very thing, that he which hath begun a good work in you will perform it until the day of Jesus Christ:" 1 John 3:2 tells us, "Beloved, now are we the sons of God, and it doth not yet appear what we shall be: but we know that, when he shall appear, we shall be like him; for we shall see him as he is." In this life, a transformed mind brings peace and joy that can only come from embracing the mind of Christ.

This chapter is short for a reason. We don't need to belabor the point because it is just what it is. It's time to Go! Begin (or continue) to give your body and mind to Christ. Start thinking like Jesus and you will know exactly where God wants you. Do you have it? You know where God wants you? If not, keep working on it. You'll get there, just don't give up! If yes, what are you waiting on? BOOK YOUR TICKET!

Pray Through

"Delight thyself also in the Lord; and he shall give thee the desires of thine heart. Commit thy way unto the Lord; trust also in him; and he shall bring it to pass." (Psalm 37:4-5)

CHAPTER 12

Final Destination

"into his harvest"
— MATTHEW 9:38 —

Welcome aboard flight #6145, with service to Cincinnati, Paris, France, and our final destination, Mumbai, India.

The final destination for the Christian, in this life, is to be involved in the harvest of the Lord. Though you may have already settled on a specific place, like India, or a specific area, like youth ministry, it is to the place of God's choosing to which we must strive daily to arrive. God has a place in His harvest for you to work. Have you found that place?

A slum: The slums are comprised of rows of make-shift dwellings, made of scrap wood, metal and cardboard, which are homes for hundreds of thousands of people - many of them children. Here are kids who grow up with no chance of changing their status in life. It has been determined by their status at birth that they are to live by the waterway that carries all the sewage from the city that is home to millions of people. This represents the cultural estimate of the worth of these populations. In the slums, the concept of good hygiene does not exist. The residents of these slums see the world around them as their bathroom and use it accordingly, much like the dogs, pigs, cattle, and other animals that live among them. Young girls that grow up with sexual abuse being the norm and young boys who are taught it is ok to treat girls that way. There is nothing wrong with it they are taught. But, saddest of all, kids who have no idea there is a Savior that loves them and gave His life for them that they may have the hope of eternal life through Him. To Jesus, they are of great value, more precious than gold or silver.

We stopped and looked at one of the dwellings that was being used as a meeting place for a Grace club. At the club, the kids were being educated and also taught about the many subjects mentioned above, especially about Jesus. I can tell you, we have better dwellings for our pets and livestock than these kids have to live and learn in. The club sat empty, not because it was an off day for them, but because there were no finances to keep it going. But there are men like Pastor Wilson who believe and trust the Lord will provide what is needed because this faithful Pastor knows this is his "final destination", the part of the harvest God has called him to.

A remote tribal area: The people build these villages, their homes among the trees using thatch cut and gleaned from the forest. Although they build their own homes, the people in these tribal areas maintain no ownership rights to the forest area they now call home and may be forcibly removed by the government at any time for any reason. This is a people group whose lives are sustained by resources found in the forest and mountains surrounding them. Their life is sustained from God's creation and yet they have no knowledge of the God of creation. Here are people holding on to a hope of a better life - whatever that may be.

I noticed there were many kids among the band of people who greeted us. As we walked up the dirt path over rocks and roots, I was struck by the beauty of the forest, the mountains and the smiling though somewhat unsure faces of the kids. Reaching the village, I saw all around me their struggle to just exist from day to day. Their struggle to provide shelter, food and the basic necessities of life became painfully real to me. I was deeply moved and could not imagine living that way. I also realized they probably could not imagine life any other way. Although we are from vastly different worlds, I also realized that the same God who loves me loves them. Because of God's great love, this tribal area is someone's "final destination". Maybe it's you – the reader of this book.

A after school club: Amongst the millions of people in this big city, a after school club is only a speck. 99.99% of the city probably didn't know it existed. I would have never known it existed if someone had not taken me there and showed it to me firsthand. Here were twenty to thirty kids, most for the first time in their life, being introduced to Jesus Christ through the avenue of educational help. Kids of all backgrounds. Church kids, non-church kids, Hindu kids, and Muslim kids. What a thrill it was to hear them, all of them, sing about Jesus and quote scripture from God's Word. Someone's "final destination" is a life impacting, life changing club which you are probably reading about for the first time.

Orphan Care: YES Ministries has been working in youth ministry in some form since 2009. Though we have done some work in India, I would say our "final destination" has been predominantly throughout the southern Caribbean region. We have done team trips to Grenada and St. Lucia and have spoken in both St. Vincent and Trinidad & Tobago as well as helping with other projects financially. God started the process of preparing me for this destination when I was nineteen years old and took my first missions trip to the island of Grenada. I didn't know it then, but God had a plan for me in this area of the world that would also affect people in my community and around the world (like in India). One of our greatest desires has been to help and serve children who have been orphaned for one reason or another. I am thankful to say that God is beginning to move our ministry in this direction. As of the writing of this book, YES Ministries is working to establish our first Children's Home on the island of St. Vincent. We pray that we will soon be serving orphaned kids at Covenant House of St. Vincent and then through other homes throughout the Caribbean as God allows.

After Jesus resurrected, He spent forty days appearing to different people, but mostly to His disciples. He talked to them about the fact that He was going to be returning to heaven. It was not surprising that His disciples had a lot of questions. What is going to happen next? Is

Jesus going to set up His kingdom now? Jesus, quite directly, told them not to worry about it, that they didn't need to know. Then in Acts 1:8, He told them what they did need to know. It is what we need to know, or be reminded of, today as well.

> "But ye shall receive power, after that the
> Holy Ghost is come upon you:
> and ye shall be witnesses unto me both in
> Jerusalem, and in all Judaea, and in Samaria,
> and unto the uttermost part of the earth."

Jesus told the disciples that they would receive power. After He returned to heaven, the Holy Ghost would come and dwell in them. The same is true today. When a person receives Jesus as Saviour, immediately the Holy Ghost (who is God) comes to live in them. Try to wrap your brain around that! It's amazing! That in itself shows the great power of God that He can dwell inside each person who believes. Matthew 28:18b says, "All power is given unto me in heaven and in earth." Don't hesitate to get into the harvest. The God who has ALL the power that there is, lives inside of you if you are His. There is nothing that you and I cannot do with that power working in us.

Jesus continues to tell the disciples that they WILL BE witnesses for Him. I wonder if they recalled when Jesus told them He would make them fishers of men if they followed Him (see Matthew 4:19 and Mark 1:17)? The question is, what kind of witness will you and I be? We will be witnesses of Jesus, but will we be good witnesses or bad witnesses? Every day, we are witnesses for Christ in some way. We are witnesses in front of our family, at our work or school, at the grocery store, on social media, everywhere we go. It is important that we remember this and work hard, and ask God to give us the strength, to be the kind of witnesses for Him that He wants us to be.

Jesus finishes up this verse by telling the disciples where they will be witnesses for Him. He starts with Jerusalem. Put your hometown here. Jesus tells them they will minister right in their hometown and so will we. No matter where God takes you, your hometown will always be at the center of where you serve. Your hometown is where God will begin to train and grow you. It is where you will have your first opportunities to serve as witnesses for Jesus. It is where the burden and desire that God gives you will first take root. I am so thankful that God gave me a burden for youth and allowed us to start YES Ministries and He began that in Bargersville, Indiana. What about you? Where has God started you on your journey to your final destination? Maybe your final destination is right there in your hometown.

You will be witnesses "in all Judaea." Judaea would represent your country. As you minister in your hometown, God may begin to put a burden on your heart for another area of the country you live in. There are several organizations in the USA that do 7-10 day mission trips throughout the country. Look into participating in one of those in an area you want to pray about ministering in. If you live outside the USA, research organizations in your country that might offer these types of opportunities. What is God laying on your heart? Maybe it is inner city ministry, working with youth or the homeless. Maybe God is leading you to minister to our Native American population on a reservation out West. Maybe you're being lead to be a Pastor in a rural area. Maybe an Evangelist, travelling the whole country preaching the Word of God. It could be God is directing you into Camp ministry or a sports ministry. You could minister to our brave men and women in the Armed Forces. The opportunities are endless because the harvest is so vast and it is plenteous. Maybe one of these areas is your final destination or maybe God just uses one of these opportunities to prepare and grow you on the way to your final destination.

Remember Samaria? That place no Jew wanted to step foot in, but Jesus said it was necessary to "go through" (John 4:4). Maybe that is where God is preparing you to go, that place where you would say anywhere but there. Don't underestimate the love God can put in your heart for a place or people group that you might think you hate. The Jews hated the Samaritans and vice versa, but Jesus broke through that hatred and through His love brought peace, joy, and eternal life. Jesus opens the door for the disciples then, and for us today, so we have the blessing of entering in those areas. Pick up a copy of the book,

Operation World: When We Pray God Works by Patrick Johnstone and Jason Mandryk. Operation World gives you information and statistics for every country in the world. This could guide you in finding your Samaria or the last place Jesus says we will be witnesses for Him.

"and unto the uttermost part of the earth." Basically, what Jesus was saying is, even those places that you have no idea even exist. My first thought went to the remote tribal areas we visited in India and also the after school clubs hidden deep inside a slum that no one would ever find if they didn't live there (and even then it's not guaranteed you will find it). Maybe God is using you in your hometown and preparing you for somewhere you've never heard of. Maybe it's Andorra in Europe or Benin in Africa. What about Niue in the Cook Islands or Timor Leste in Asia? Wherever it is, even though right now it doesn't even exist to you, be open if this is where God wants you. He will prepare you. He will give you the tools you need for the job. He will give you the strength to endure and the love to share. He will give you, well, everything! Where will your final destination be? I don't know for sure other than it is somewhere in the middle of the harvest. Enjoy your journey. Enjoy your perfect destination. Welcome aboard!

Pray Through

"Therefore I will look unto the Lord; I will wait for the God of my salvation: my God will hear me." (Micah 7:7)

CONCLUSION

I prefer the…? What's your choice? Aisle or Window? It's not an easy choice, but it is simple. It really just comes down to, will I do what God wants (aisle) or am I going to do what I want (window)? Most Christians would say, I really want to do what God wants. Or at least they used to. I'm not sure that is the case with today's American Christian. I believe it is more like, I want to do what God wants, but I want to do what I want more. God has to work with my plans. I read about Christian men and women of old, who risked everything to take the Gospel to unreached peoples, most losing their lives for the call of Christ. Where have those Christians gone? I hear today of Christians in far-a-way lands who are persecuted and killed, their heads cut off, their families slain, homes, churches, burnt to the ground simply for following Jesus and through these tragedies, more follow Jesus. Not so in America. What the American church has done is convince members that participation means involvement. We've told ourselves this lie over and over and over again until we actually believe it now. But, we know it's not true. What do I mean? If you ignore the truth, you can convince yourself it's not there. If you sit in the window seat, you can actually convince yourself that the chaos in the aisle isn't really there. So, what is the truth? This is probably not the first time you have heard or read this portion of scripture in Matthew 9. It is one of those portions of scripture that is quoted or used a lot, especially in Mission Conferences. You have probably prayed, with good intentions, that God would send people to the harvest. They may have gone something like this. God, that Missionaries story was really sad. Please send them help. Johnny would be good for that job or man, that seems like a good fit for Sally. Lord lay that on their heart. Or, maybe you prayed, God, I'll do whatever you want as long as you don't send me to another country. Or, maybe you have even prayed the bold prayer I have before. Lord, here is what I want to do, make that work (maybe not verbatim, but definitely the gist)! What have we done? We totally ignored Matthew 10. It's not even there! Let me explain. Jesus told the disciples to pray in Matthew 9:38. Pray for labourers to be sent. I believe they probably said ok and then prayed. And, what was the result of their prayers? Read below Matthew 10 – 11:1:

10 And when he had called unto him his twelve disciples, he gave them power against unclean spirits, to cast them out, and to heal all manner of sickness and all manner of disease.

² Now the names of the twelve apostles are these; The first, Simon, who is called Peter, and Andrew his brother; James the son of Zebedee, and John his brother;

³ Philip, and Bartholomew; Thomas, and Matthew the publican; James the son of Alphaeus, and Lebbaeus, whose surname was Thaddaeus;

⁴ Simon the Canaanite, and Judas Iscariot, who also betrayed him.

⁵ These twelve Jesus sent forth, and commanded them, saying, Go not into the way of the Gentiles, and into any city of the Samaritans enter ye not:

⁶ But go rather to the lost sheep of the house of Israel.

⁷ And as ye go, preach, saying, The kingdom of heaven is at hand.

⁸ Heal the sick, cleanse the lepers, raise the dead, cast out devils: freely ye have received, freely give.

⁹ Provide neither gold, nor silver, nor brass in your purses,

¹⁰ Nor scrip for your journey, neither two coats, neither shoes, nor yet staves: for the workman is worthy of his meat.

¹¹ And into whatsoever city or town ye shall enter, enquire who in it is worthy; and there abide till ye go thence.

¹² And when ye come into an house, salute it.

¹³ And if the house be worthy, let your peace come upon it: but if it be not worthy, let your peace return to you.

[14] And whosoever shall not receive you, nor hear your words, when ye depart out of that house or city, shake off the dust of your feet.

[15] Verily I say unto you, It shall be more tolerable for the land of Sodom and Gomorrha in the day of judgment, than for that city.

[16] Behold, I send you forth as sheep in the midst of wolves: be ye therefore wise as serpents, and harmless as doves.

[17] But beware of men: for they will deliver you up to the councils, and they will scourge you in their synagogues;

[18] And ye shall be brought before governors and kings for my sake, for a testimony against them and the Gentiles.

[19] But when they deliver you up, take no thought how or what ye shall speak: for it shall be given you in that same hour what ye shall speak.

[20] For it is not ye that speak, but the Spirit of your Father which speaketh in you.

[21] And the brother shall deliver up the brother to death, and the father the child: and the children shall rise up against their parents, and cause them to be put to death.

[22] And ye shall be hated of all men for my name's sake: but he that endureth to the end shall be saved.

[23] But when they persecute you in this city, flee ye into another: for verily I say unto you, Ye shall not have gone over the cities of Israel, till the Son of man be come.

[24] The disciple is not above his master, nor the servant above his lord.

[25] It is enough for the disciple that he be as his master, and the servant as his lord. If they have called the master of the house Beelzebub, how much more shall they call them of his household?

[26] Fear them not therefore: for there is nothing covered, that shall not be revealed; and hid, that shall not be known.

[27] What I tell you in darkness, that speak ye in light: and what ye hear in the ear, that preach ye upon the housetops.

[28] And fear not them which kill the body, but are not able to kill the soul: but rather fear him which is able to destroy both soul and body in hell.

²⁹ Are not two sparrows sold for a farthing? and one of them shall not fall on the ground without your Father.

³⁰ But the very hairs of your head are all numbered.

³¹ Fear ye not therefore, ye are of more value than many sparrows.

³² Whosoever therefore shall confess me before men, him will I confess also before my Father which is in heaven.

³³ But whosoever shall deny me before men, him will I also deny before my Father which is in heaven.

³⁴ Think not that I am come to send peace on earth: I came not to send peace, but a sword.

³⁵ For I am come to set a man at variance against his father, and the daughter against her mother, and the daughter in law against her mother in law.

³⁶ And a man's foes shall be they of his own household.

³⁷ He that loveth father or mother more than me is not worthy of me: and he that loveth son or daughter more than me is not worthy of me.

³⁸ And he that taketh not his cross, and followeth after me, is not worthy of me.

³⁹ He that findeth his life shall lose it: and he that loseth his life for my sake shall find it.

⁴⁰ He that receiveth you receiveth me, and he that receiveth me receiveth him that sent me.

⁴¹ He that receiveth a prophet in the name of a prophet shall receive a prophet's reward; and he that receiveth a righteous man in the name of a righteous man shall receive a righteous man's reward.

⁴² And whosoever shall give to drink unto one of these little ones a cup of cold water only in the name of a disciple, verily I say unto you, he shall in no wise lose his reward.

11 And it came to pass, when Jesus had made an end of commanding his twelve disciples, he departed thence to teach and to preach in their cities.

Did you see it? Who did God send? Yep, the Apostles. The very ones who prayed. There is a quote that says, "As so often occurs, those who prayed were themselves sent." Our prayers have changed because our hearts have changed. We no longer pray, Lord, here am I, send me. Now we pray, Lord, Here am I, send Bill. Jesus didn't ask us to pray for Bill to be sent. He wants us to pray with a heart that says if it is me you send, that's great, I'll go. But, we don't want to pray that. Why? Read Matthew 10 again. Who would willingly sign up for that life? Oh yeah, only someone who has been radically changed by Jesus. Only the person that prays, God, where do you want me to "sit"? God, please show me my "final destination". God, I'm "booking my ticket". There is an alarming shift in American Christianity. We no longer want to be radically changed (involved). Now, we just want to be radically comfortable (participate). Matthew chapter 10 shows us what it looks like to be involved, to sit in the aisle seat. Don't be afraid to jump in the aisle seat. When you sit there, you will never sit there alone. Take comfort in that and go forth with boldness. Go reach those that God has prepared for you. Take the message of the Gospel and bring comfort to a world that is hurting, joy to a world that is joyless, hope to a world that is hopeless, light to a world that is dark, life to a world that is dead, and love to a world that is broken. My challenge to you, and to me is, jump in the aisle seat and see what God will do. I know your response will be that of the Psalmist in Psalm 91:2, ***"I will say of the Lord, He is my refuge and my fortress: my God; in him will I trust."*** (Emphasis mine)

Pray Through

"Commit thy works unto the Lord, and thy thoughts shall be established." (Proverbs 16:3)

May the Lord bless you in your field, wherever that may be, and my prayers will be with you as you labor for the Lord in this great and plenteous harvest.

Tony

Printed in the United States
By Bookmasters